RIVERS
of the
WORLD

The Rhine

Titles in the Rivers of the World series include:

The Amazon
The Ganges
The Mississippi
The Nile
The Rhine

RIVERS
～ of the ～
WORLD

The Rhine

Stuart A. Kallen

**LUCENT
BOOKS®**

THOMSON
━━━━✦━━━━
™

San Diego • Detroit • New York • Sa   Waterville, Maine • London • Munich

On Cover: A glass-sided passenger boat docks along
the Rhine River near Düsseldorf, Germany.

LIBRARY OF CONGRESS CATALOGING-IN-PUBLICATION DATA

Kallen, Stuart A., 1955–
    The Rhine / by Stuart A. Kallen.
    p. cm. — (Rivers of the world series)
    Summary: Describes the Rhine River from ancient times to the present, and discusses
what must be done to protect and preserve this river.
    Includes bibliographical references and index.
        ISBN 1-59018-062-3 (hardback : alk. paper)
        1. Rhine River—Juvenile literature. 2. Rhine River—Description and travel—Juvenile
literature. [1. Rhine River.] I. Title. II. Rivers of the world (Lucent Books)
        DD801 .R74 K28 2003
        943'.4—dc21
                                                        2002011051

Printed in the United States of America

Contents

• • • • • • • • • • • • •

Foreword

Human history and rivers are inextricably intertwined. Of all the geologic wonders of nature, none has played a more central and continuous role in the history of civilization than rivers. Fanning out across every major landmass except the Antarctic, all great rivers wove an arterial network that played a pivotal role in the inception of early civilizations and in the evolution of today's modern nation-states.

More than ten thousand years ago, when nomadic tribes first began to settle into small, stable communities, they discovered the benefits of cultivating crops and domesticating animals. These incipient civilizations developed a dependence on continuous flows of water to nourish and sustain their communities and food supplies. As small agrarian towns began to dot the Asian and African continents, the importance of rivers escalated as sources of community drinking water, as places for washing clothes, for sewage removal, for food, and as means of transportation. One by one, great riparian civilizations evolved whose collective fame is revered today, including ancient Mesopotamia, between the Tigris and Euphrates Rivers; Egypt, along the Nile; India, along the Ganges and Indus Rivers; and China, along the Yangtze. Later, for the same reasons, early civilizations in the Americas gravitated to the major rivers of the New World such as the Amazon, Mississippi, and Colorado.

For thousands of years, these rivers admirably fulfilled their role in nature's cycle of birth, death, and renewal. The waters also supported the rise of nations and their expanding populations. As hundreds and then thousands of cities sprang up along major rivers, today's modern nations emerged and discovered modern uses for the rivers. With more mouths to feed than ever before, great irrigation canals supplied by river water fanned out across the landscape, transforming parched land into mile upon mile of fertile cropland. Engineers developed the mathematics needed to throw great concrete dams across rivers to control occasional flooding and to store trillions of gallons of water to irrigate crops during the hot summer months. When the great age of electricity arrived, engineers added to the demands placed on rivers by using their cascading water to drive huge hydroelectric turbines to light and heat homes and skyscrapers in urban settings. Rivers also played a major role in the development of modern factories as sources of water for processing a variety of commercial goods and as a convenient place to discharge various types of refuse.

For a time, civilizations and rivers functioned in harmony. Such a benign relationship, however, was not destined to last. At the end of the twentieth century, scientists confirmed the opinions of environmentalists: The viability of all major rivers of the world was threatened. Urban populations could no longer drink the fetid water, masses of fish were dying from chemical toxins, and microorganisms critical to the food chain were disappearing along with the fish species at the top of the chain. The great hydroelectric dams had altered the natural flow of rivers, blocking migratory fish routes. As the twenty-first century unfolds, all who have contributed to spoiling the rivers are now in agreement that immediate steps must be taken to heal the rivers if their partnership with civilization is to continue.

Each volume in the Lucent Rivers of the World series tells the unique and fascinating story of a great river and its people. The significance of rivers to civilizations is emphasized to highlight both their historical role and the present situation. Each volume illustrates the idiosyncrasies of one great river in terms of its physical attributes, the plants and animals that depend on it, its role in ancient and modern cultures, how it served the needs of the people, the misuse of the river, and steps now being taken to remedy its problems.

Introduction

• • • • • • • • • • • • • • • • • •

The Highway of Europe

The Rhine is one of the most important rivers in Europe, flowing north from Switzerland, connecting Austria, Liechtenstein, France, and Germany, and draining into the North Sea in the Netherlands. At 820 miles in length, the Rhine is not the longest European river, but it is the busiest. With 50 million people living near its waters, the Rhine has long been at the heart of European civilization, and many great cities, including Basel, Strasbourg, Frankfurt, Cologne, Düsseldorf, and Rotterdam, have grown up along its banks. Today the river supports a broad range of activities including shipping, tourism, agriculture, and industry.

Human interaction with the Rhine is only part of the river's story. Thousands of years before people ever arrived in the Rhine Valley, the river environment supported hundreds of animal species. And along its banks varied ecosystems flourished, including mountain meadows, pine forests, and lush wetlands that hosted a broad range of wildlife.

Ripe with natural resources, it was inevitable that the Rhine would attract humans to its environs. Since the river rarely freezes and its waters have always been abun-

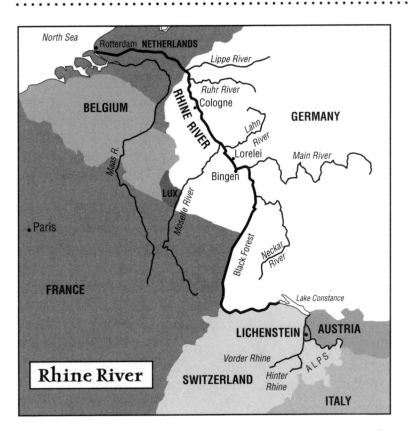

dant, even the earliest settlers used the Rhine as a trade route. By the Middle Ages it was the busiest river in Europe. And almost as quickly as its waters brought wealth and well-being to its citizens, the Rhine became a source of conflict. Various tribes squabbled over access to its waters, and well into the twentieth century, nations battled each other for control of what they considered a strategically vital waterway.

Though many countries and cultures have fought over the Rhine, its name has remained nearly the same throughout history, reflecting its Latin root. The early Germanic word for the river, *Rhein* or *Rein* is, in English, "run" as in "flow." To early Celts it was Renos; to the Romans it was Rhenus. The Italians refer to it as Reno, the French, Rhin. In modern Germany the importance of the river is noted in the common phrase "Vater Rhein," or "Father Rhine." No matter the language, the Rhine has always been revered as a body of water from which life itself flows.

Although millions have taken sustenance from the Rhine, few civilizations living along its banks have returned the kindness. Even in the Middle Ages complaints about the stench of the polluted water were common among people living along the river. From its earliest days the river has been used as a receptacle for human, animal, and industrial waste. Since the mid-nineteenth century the Rhine has been one of the most industrialized rivers in Europe, and today some stretches of the Rhine are virtually dead: In these waters no fish or other wildlife can survive. Other parts of the river have been cleaned up and fish have returned to the waters. And many miles of the Upper Rhine remain scenic and even pristine.

Despite the increasingly obvious pollution, over the years the Rhine inspired artists, authors, and composers to celebrate its beauty in paintings, poems, and song. Perhaps the most famous work centered on the river is German composer Richard Wagner's *Das Rheingold* (*The Rhinegold*), a monumental opera about a powerful ring made of gold taken from the Rhine—a ring whose beauty causes misery to those who desire it and fight over it.

In this work and others, the Rhine is often immortalized as a symbol of both good and evil—a powerful river whose waters grant life but whose occasional floods can deliver massive destruction; a river that supports thriving villages and cities but whose strategic importance attracts armies that destroy those settlements in battles of conquest; a river whose natural beauty attracted humans whose activities threatened to destroy that splendor.

Over the centuries, the river has fulfilled the very practical purpose of being a natural dividing line between several nations. Yet today the Rhine has served to unite European nations that were once sworn enemies. Countries that fought one another throughout the centuries are now committed to work together at cleaning up

Fishing on the Rhine. Parts of the Rhine remain scenic, despite centuries of industrialization along the river.

the Rhine and restoring the river to its former greatness. These countries have also agreed to peacefully share the bounty of the Rhine. Where battles once raged, cooperation is now the watchword.

For as long as the Rhine has flowed through human settlements, its waters have reflected the will of its people. From its source in the high mountain springs of the Alps to its delta at the sea, the Rhine continues to act as a main artery to a continent, bringing life and renewal to the heart of Europe.

1
· · · · · · · · · ·

Flowing Through Europe

High in the Swiss Alps some ten thousand years ago, glaciers formed what today is known as Lake Constance. Melting ice and snow filled that lake to overflowing with cold, calm, clear water. The overflow from the lake created a tumbling river that cascaded downhill until, finding its way through valleys and plains, it finally emptied into the sea.

As the last Ice Age ended, the glaciers retreated to the coldest, highest mountain elevations where they are replenished year after year by new snow. As these glaciers melt, the resulting runoff feeds the headwaters of the Rhine.

The Alpine Rhine

In the eastern Swiss canton, or district, of Grisons, snow-capped mountains rise over eleven thousand feet above sea level. On the towering Marscholhorn peak, near St. Bernard pass, the icy Rheinwaldhorn glacier slowly melts when the weather warms in the spring and summer. In a small opening in the ice, sixteen feet high and forty-nine feet wide, the first cold, calm, muddy waters of the Rhine emerge. The stream here, known as the Hinterrhein, or Farther Rhine, is about thirty-three feet wide and, as it plunges downhill through rugged canyons, it is fed by dozens of small creeks whose waters also derive from the melting snow and glaciers of the Alps.

Monk Gibbon poetically describes this part of the river in *The Rhine and Its Castles*: "Here in the Canton de Grisons, the Rhine is young, violent, excitable, irresponsible, the scent of pine trees in its nostrils, and the heady elation of recent escape from the region of snows helping to hasten it on its way."[1]

The Hinterrhein falls rapidly after leaving the glacier, plunging more than two thousand feet within ten miles. Nobody can navigate this stream, and even walking along it can be a death-defying feat. The thirty-foot-wide, black slate gorge through which it flows for three and a half miles is so steep and dangerous it is known as Via Mala, or the "Evil Way," a name given to it two thousand years ago by the Romans, whose soldiers sometimes plunged to their deaths while attempting to negotiate the canyon trails that clung to the sheer sides of the canyon.

A waterfall in the Swiss Alps. Annual runoff from glaciers high in the Swiss Alps creates the headwaters of the Rhine River.

The young, turbulent river slows as it enters the Rheinwald Valley, a flat plain where the small, picturesque village of Hinterrhein marks the first outpost of civilization along the river's banks. Despite the presence of thousands of summer tourists, life has changed little here since the village was first founded in the thirteenth century. People continue to scratch out a living in the cold mountain climate, tending sheep, goats, and cows in the pastures of the valley.

Alpine Beginnings

The Rhine begins life in the towering Swiss Alps, a beautiful mountain setting that has long inspired poetic descriptions of the river, such as this one by Felizia Seyd in The Rhine:

All mountain-born rivers sing but their melody is clearest near the source where the river is alone with ice, rock, and the sky. [So too with] the Rhine, whose voice becomes muted in its course through the plains [in lower elevations] but rings out clearly in the mountain wildernesses where it is born. And the voice, from the start, [resembles] the river's temper. Harsh, impatient, and even threatening in parts, then again gentle, submissive, and serene, it expresses a will to survive and a need for dramatic achievement.

It is only a few hours' walk from the nearest Swiss village to the source of the...Rhine, but it is a wearisome path, leading uphill through a canyonlike valley flanked by steep barren inclines. The trail, if you can call it a trail, threads...a nest of glacier-clad peaks.... Perilous in parts, skirting here an abyss, there the end of a slippery moraine [accumulation of boulders], it climbs to an altitude of nearly eight thousand feet where rock and soil begin to yield to the hungry embrace of a low-hanging glacier. And there [the trail] ends... attaining an elevation of over eleven thousand feet.... A river is born here from the tired flanks of an exhausted glacier.

Southeast of Hinterrhein, another major tributary of the river, known as the Vorder Rhine, or Nearer Rhine, flows out of Lake Toma. The Vorder Rhine, which itself is fed by dozens of smaller streams, meets the Hinterrhein at Reichenau, about six miles south of the medieval village of Chur, the capital of Grisons canton. Past this point, the river is known as the Alpine Rhine as it flows northwest for about sixty miles through wide valleys dotted with scenic villages nestled at the feet of towering mountain peaks and rocky spires.

In this area, the Rhine forms the western border of the tiny, sixty-two-square-mile principality of Liechtenstein, one of the smallest countries in the world. The river also briefly marks the border between Austria and Switzerland before its milky glacial waters drain into the southern end of Lake Constance.

Bordered by Germany, Switzerland, and Austria, Lake Constance is about forty-two miles long and eight miles wide, and its deepest point reaches 827 feet. Thanks to its size and depth, this clear, cold lake acts as a brake for the fast-flowing waters of the Alpine Rhine, absorbing flood-waters in spring and releasing only one-tenth of the water it receives from the mountain glaciers. Throughout history, this natural reservoir has, for the most part, prevented people living downstream from being subjected to catastrophic flooding in the spring.

So effectively does Lake Constance slow the river's progress that researchers estimate that it takes an average of two months for the Rhine's waters to flow the length of the lake. When the river emerges from the

The Rhine Falls descend from Lake Constance at Schaffhausen, Switzerland, as depicted in this 1908 painting.

northern reaches, near the Swiss town of Schaffhausen, it thunders over the 75-foot-high Rhine Falls. Here the river is 488 feet wide, making this waterfall the largest in Central Europe. The waters of Rhine Falls surge at a rate of 13 million gallons a minute. While this is spectacular by European standards, it is rather modest when compared with the world's major waterfalls. For example, Niagara Falls near Buffalo, New York, contains almost six times more water and falls a distance of 187 feet, while Victoria Falls in Africa is a mile wide and plunges 360 feet.

The Rift Valley

After the Rhine passes over its greatest waterfall, it becomes a calm and gentle river that has encouraged the development of shipping and transportation industries over the years. From here to the North Sea, the Rhine is a commercial as well as scenic river, plied by barges and pleasure boats and lined with factories, farms, villages, towns, and cities.

At Basel, Switzerland, the river forms the borders of three countries—Switzerland, Germany, and France. Basel is the first major port on the Rhine. Here, through a network of canals and river tributaries, as well as on the Rhine itself, ships arrive from the Mediterranean, Black, Baltic, Caspian, White, and North Seas as well as from the Bay of Biscay on the Atlantic coast between Spain and France and the English Channel between France and England. This access to world markets has helped make Basel a major manufacturing city for pharmaceutical, textile, publishing, and other industries.

As the Rhine runs between Basel and Bingen, Germany—a distance of 180 miles—it flows through a broad, flat valley about twenty miles wide. This area is called the Rhine Rift Valley or, in German, *Graben*. (A rift is a steep-sided valley with a flat floor that exists between two fractures—called faults—in the earth's crust.)

In its natural state, the Rhine once meandered through the flat stretch between Basel and Strasbourg, France, looping back on itself and making new channels when waters were high. Today, a straight channel marked by a series of locks and dams runs west of and parallel to the Rhine, siphoning much of the river's water from its natural course. Built in the 1950s and 1960s and known as the Grand Canal d'Alsace, this waterway takes shipping traffic off the Rhine for a distance of seventy miles.

Away from the canal, the Rhine flows north, forming the border between France and Germany for 120 miles. Goronwy Rees describes the natural features of the river valley in *The Rhine*:

> The Rift valley of the Rhine, especially on its first seventy miles between Basle and Strasbourg, is both one of the most interesting and one of the most beautiful natural features of Europe. The steep slopes of the Vosges [Mountains] on the west bank and of the Black Forest [of Germany] on the east rise to a height of nearly 5,000 feet; the flat fertile bottom of the valley between them is nearly twenty miles [wide] and covered by orchards and cultivated fields which yield crops of [corn], hops, and tobacco.... [The] steep slopes of the mountains on either [side] are terraced by vineyards, which give way to a dark green ribbon of pine forests and finally to open upland pastures.[2]

As the Rhine continues its journey north, it passes through one of Germany's most renowned resort cities, Baden-Baden. Founded by the Romans in the third century, Baden-Baden is home to natural mineral hot springs. For centuries, well-to-do tourists from across Europe have come to the fashionable spas whose waters have been said to cure every ill from backaches to cancer.

North of Karlsruhe, the Rhine leaves the French-German border to become an entirely German river. After about forty miles the Rhine meets the river Neckar and the river Main, two major tributaries. This region, with its

A nineteenth-century painting shows a crowd of affluent European tourists in Baden-Baden, the German resort town along the Rhine.

many petrochemical, automotive, and engineering facilities built around the city of Mannheim on the Neckar, is the economic heart of the Upper Rhine. The city of Mainz is constructed at the confluence of the Main, and a short distance upstream is the bustling city of Frankfurt, a major commercial and financial center in central Germany.

The Rhine Gorge

It is at the confluence with the Main that the Rhine takes a ninety-degree turn to the west and enters the Rhine Gorge. Here industry disappears, and the river narrows as the Taunus Mountains rise up on either side of its banks. This fifty-mile stretch of river between Bingen and Bonn is less than six hundred feet wide in some places, and the valley is marked by sheer cliffs that jut up from the river-banks.

The scenery is most impressive between Bingen and Koblenz, where ruins of ancient castles grace the hilltops. These mighty fortresses, perched upon the highest rocky crags, were constructed in the Middle Ages by powerful local princes, who from their commanding position over-looking the river demanded that shipowners pay tolls in return for safe passage. The last tolls on ships and their cargoes were collected in 1868, but this portion of the Rhine remains a dangerous place for ships. As William Graves writes in *National Geographic*:

> One despot remains in the Rhine Gorge to this day— the fierce, intractable river itself. From early Roman times...boatmen have feared the 35-mile-long *Gebirgsstrecke*, or "mountain stretch," as the gorge is sometimes known. Clamped between the mountains' massive jaws, the river twists and writhes in its narrow bed, forever creating new currents and shoals to trap the unwary helmsman.[3]

The most hazardous stretch of the Rhine Gorge is the Binger Loch, or "Binger Hole," where a steep, slate cliff known as Lorelei rises more than 450 feet above the water. Legend has it that Lorelei, a beautiful mythical maiden, sang her songs beneath the cliff and lured sailors to their deaths on the rocks along the Rhine shores.

Past Lorelei, the Rhine Gorge widens temporarily into a broad lowland known as the Neuwied Basin. Here the Lahn and Moselle (or Mosel) Rivers join the Rhine near the ancient city of Koblenz. This is the heart of the Moselle wine region and the sheer hills along the river have been planted with grape vines since the fourth century A.D. As Stuart Pigott writes in *Touring Wine Country: The Mosel & Rheingau*: "Here vines flourish on lofty, narrow terraces and slopes so [steep] that it makes you dizzy to even look up at them from flat ground."[4]

The Deadly Song of Lorelei

For centuries, boatmen on the Rhine have feared piloting their vessels through the narrow 150-foot-wide spot in the Rhine Gorge, about halfway between Bingen and Koblenz. Here, the towering black slate cliff known as Lorelei rises 450 feet above the water.

In 1802 Clemens von Brentano wrote a poem in which he invented a beautiful maiden named Lorelei, who sat by the cliff combing her golden hair while singing songs that lured innocent sailors to their doom on the jagged rocks nearby. Since that time dozens of artists, poets, and composers have created their own works dedicated to the siren Lorelei. On the "Wilhelm Ruland. Legends of the Rhine. Lorelei." website, Ruland poetically describes the siren:

The maiden Lorelei, purveyor of doom along the Rhine.

Long, long ago…the soft voice of a woman was heard from the rock, and a creature of divine beauty was seen on its summit. Her golden locks flowed like a queenly mantle from her graceful shoulders, covering her snow white raiment so that her tenderly-formed body appeared like a cloud of light.

Woe to the boatman who passed the rock at the close of day! As of old, men were fascinated by the heavenly song of [Lorelei], so was the unhappy voyager allured by this Being to sweet forgetfulness, his eyes, even his soul, would be dazzled, and he could no longer steer clear of reefs and cliffs, and this beautiful siren only drew him to an early grave. Forgetting all else, he would steer towards her, already dreaming of having reached her; but the jealous waves would round his boat and at last dash him treacherously against the rocks. The roaring waters of the Rhine would drown the cries of agony and the victim would never be seen again.

The Lower Rhine

As the Rhine continues its journey north, the gorge ends where the river enters the Lower Rhine Plain. Before the flat basin begins, however, a group of wooded ridges and peaks, called Siebengebirge, or Seven Mountains, rises up on the east side of the Rhine and follows the river for about ten miles. These remnants of ancient volcanoes, some as high as fifteen hundred feet, are steeped in legend.

The fairy tale of Snow White is said to have been set in a nearby castle. And the highest of the Seven Mountains, Drachenfels, or Dragon Rock, is where a brave young man named Siegfried is said to have slain a dragon. The hills are also mentioned in the German legend of the Nibelungs, an ancient tale of gods, giants, humans, and dwarves called Nibelungs. Richard Wagner based his epic opera cycle *The Ring of the Nibelung* on this story. Today, the area has become a prime destination for tourists, and large crowds utilize the hills for hiking, picnics, and other recreational activities.

Flowing north from the Seven Hills the river passes the city of Bonn, birthplace of composer Ludwig van Beethoven and capital of West Germany from 1949 to 1990. From this point to the Netherlands border, the Rhine flows through gently rolling, open country containing one of the largest concentrations of population and industrial production in Europe, with steel mills, coal mines, textile plants, refineries, and other factories lining the shore.

In the northernmost region of this area, where the Ruhr River meets the Rhine, veins of coal located close to the surface have made this an important mining and steel-making region. At the confluence of the Ruhr, the largest inland port in the world can be found in the city of Duisburg, where wharves, docks, and shipyards line a solid twenty miles of Rhine riverbank. And the area between Bonn and Duisburg, known as the Rhine-Ruhr district, is one of the most densely populated parts of Europe, containing the cities of Cologne, Düsseldorf, and smaller towns that are so close together that there are no distinct boundaries between them. Within this Rhine-Ruhr megalopolis the population exceeds 11 million.

Here the Rhine works the hardest as a watery highway. Warehouses, grain silos, steel mills, railroad yards, junk-yards, factories, and shipyards line the banks of the river. Huge barges chug up and down loaded with new automobiles, farm machinery, livestock, giant rolls of paper, engines, auto parts, scrap metal, and raw materials such as industrial chemicals, coal, iron ore, and oil.

The Rhine Delta

While the Rhine-Ruhr district is heavily industrialized, it is also contained within a sharply defined area. A few miles north of Duisburg the line of factories ends abruptly and the banks of the Rhine are once again lined with pastures, farms, and small villages.

After the German town of Emmerich, the river passes into the Netherlands, also known as Holland. Here, as the Rhine runs the last miles to the sea, it is not one river but many branches flowing through low delta lands. The Dutch call each branch of the Rhine by a different name—the Waal, the Maas (or Meuse), the Lek, the Old Rhine, the Crooked Rhine, and the Lower Rhine—but all receive water that comes from the Rhine itself. As Goronwy Rees describes it:

> [Having] crossed the Dutch frontier at Emmerich [the Rhine] almost immediately divides into a number of channels in which its identity is lost. Just as, on its upper reaches in Switzerland, it collects the waters of innumerable streams, uniting them into a single great river, so after leaving Germany it discharges them through an intricate pattern of separate channels to the sea. If the Rhine has no single beginning, so also it has no single end.[5]

The two main channels are the Lek and the Waal. The Lek flows west to the port city of Rotterdam and enters the North Sea by the New Waterway Canal. The Waal merges with the Maas to form the Merwede, which also flows into the North Sea, west of the Lek. The Crooked Rhine flows to the town of Utrecht after which it is known as the Old Rhine. This branch is linked to Amsterdam by the Amsterdam-Rhine Canal and then by the North Sea Canal to the North Sea. As William Graves writes, the Rhine in the Netherlands "is like a hand with fingers spread across the west of Holland. . . . When [in] Germany, all the fingers [are] drawn together on a single arm."[6]

The Waal River (pictured) merges with the Maas in the Rhine Delta, just before emptying into the North Sea.

More than a quarter of the Netherlands lies below sea level on land reclaimed from the Rhine and two other rivers. This poses special problems for the almost 10 million people who live in areas below sea level. From the earliest settlement, the Dutch have been fighting off the high tides of the North Sea and the floodwaters of the Rhine with earthen dikes and canals. In the twentieth century the Dutch channeled the Rhine into a series of concrete canals and used electric pumps to keep the lowlands dry.

Major floods have been a way of life in the Netherlands, but the country has also benefited from its proximity to the Rhine River. The rich soil that has been deposited there by the river over the centuries has been ideal for agricultural purposes, especially growing tulips, a popular export product of the Netherlands.

The landscape along the various Rhine branches is starkly different from the industrial scenes upstream in Germany. Woodlands, marshes, sand hills, and pastures filled with grazing livestock flank the channels through the Netherlands.

The final city on the Rhine, Rotterdam, is just down-stream from the confluence of the Maas and the Lek. Rotterdam is one of the busiest ports in the world and is the center for shipping from Europe to the rest of the world.

The end of the Nieuwe Maas is known as Hoek van Holland, and here, amid desolate sand dunes, the liquid highway of central Europe ends its long and varied jour-

Life Below Sea Level

The Netherlands is about the size of Massachusetts and Connecticut combined. The country lies on a low river delta, and the threat of floods is constant. Since the first people moved to the Netherlands about two thousand years ago, they have been struggling to keep their heads above water. In The History of Holland, *Mark T. Hooker explains the Dutch dilemma:*

Holland literally means "land in a hollow." About 27% of the country is below sea level, and that is where about 60% of the population lives. The average elevation is only...37 feet above sea level. Holland is so low because it lies in the deltas of three rivers—the Rhine...the Meuse... and the Scheldt...where they flow into the North Sea.... In addition to its rivers, Holland has one of Europe's most extensive networks of canals. Because there is water everywhere you go, swimming is a required sub-

ject in grade school as a practical safety measure for children....

The lowest point in the country is...22 feet below sea level in the Prince Alexander Polder—"polder" is the word the Dutch use for land reclaimed from under the sea.... In the west, the flat Dutch landscape is crisscrossed with drainage ditches that help keep the lowlands dry. The windmills—first used in the thirteenth century—that used to stand at the ends of these checkerboards to pump the water out, have been replaced by smaller and less obvious electric pumps that often run on solar cells. The windmills that used to drive the pumps and grind grain are now tourist attractions and museums....

The fight to keep the lowlands above water has been long and hard.... They had to learn to swim together or, most assuredly, they would have all drowned separately.

A bridge spans the Maas River at Rotterdam, the final city on the Rhine.

ney. On its path to the sea, the Rhine flows through gorges, wide valleys, major cities, past factories, cathedrals, castles, and ancient ruins. As Monk Gibbon writes:

> Just as the life of the human individual passes through a number of different phases or epochs, so does the life of the Rhine. Sometimes it has a gentle, rural, almost deserted air, flanked by meadows and graceful willow trees, and sundered by long, narrow, green, leafy islets, which appear to float upon its surface. Sometimes its banks shake with the vibrations of traffic and, everywhere the eye turns, there seems to be some form or other of watercraft hastening silently upon its way. It has not one port but many...and, as well as...great cities, countless smaller towns and villages have a reason to feel grateful to the [Father] Rhine.[7]

2

History and Conflict Along the Rhine

As one of the major waterways of central Europe, the Rhine has been at the axis of conflict from the first days of human habitation. Almost every famous conqueror in history including Julius Caesar, Charlemagne, Napoléon, and Adolf Hitler has shed blood over control of the Rhine. And great civilizations rose and fell along its banks, each one seeking to control the riches of the remarkable river. Yet there is much more to the history of the Rhineland than conflict and war.

The banks of the Rhine are built from extremely fertile soil deposited by the river's waters over the millennia. Throughout the centuries, this rich earth supported a wide variety of agricultural crops. The riverbank woodlands and meadows supplied trees for building and wild animals whose meat and skins provided food and clothing. And the fish that thrived in the river Rhine provided sustenance for people across Europe.

Lake Constance Pile Dwellings

The first humans to depend on the Rhine for their livelihoods were hunters and gatherers who, around 8000 B.C., built the first permanent settlements on the shores of Lake Constance. These villages consisted of houses called "pile dwellings" built over the shallow wetlands near the lakeshore. These structures provided easy access to a variety of foods including fowl, fish, and wetland vegetables such as cattails and other foods.

Pile dwellings were constructed over tree trunks, or piles, pounded into the lake bed. On top of the piles, board

A Celt from the Roman period (wielding sword). The Celts were the first major settlers along the Rhine.

platforms made from split trees were fastened on top of crossbeams and held in place by wooden pins. The walls of the huts were made from wattle—that is, twigs, reeds, and branches woven together and coated with clay.

Entire settlements with dozens of huts were built in this manner by the early settlers in the Alpine Rhine region. The structures were connected by gangways and bridges, and villages were accessed by canoes carved from hollowed logs. Remnants of at least thirty-two villages of pile dwellings have been identified along Lake Constance.

Around 5000 B.C., tribes from the Balkan region to the southeast began moving into the Rhine Valley in present-day western Germany. These people lived in caves and huts and sustained themselves by hunting, fishing, and gathering herbs, fruits, and vegetables from the wilderness.

The Celts

By 800 B.C. the Rhineland was populated by the Celts, the first major culture to settle along the river. The Celts were farmers and warriors who would rule much of central and western Europe, Ireland, and Great Britain for more than eight hundred years.

By the fifth century the Celts controlled the Rhine as well as other major European rivers such as the Rhone and the Danube. Meanwhile, a distinctive Celtic culture, known to archaeologists as La Tene, developed along the Middle Rhine. This group of Celts was known for its artwork, which utilized distinctive abstract geometric designs in bird and animal forms made from iron, bronze, silver, and gold.

The Celts sailed up and down the Rhine while aggressively expanding the territory they controlled. In the process they pillaged towns and villages throughout Europe. Around 390 B.C. they invaded and sacked Rome and southern Italy all the way down to Sicily. From their base along the Rhine they sent warring parties to Delphi in Greece in 279 B.C. and even crossed into present-day Turkey the following year to plunder and loot.

The Celts remained strong until around 70 B.C., when the Batavi tribes from the Rhine delta in present-day Netherlands began to push southward into the region. These invaders displaced the Celts, who were forced to flee westward. These newcomers took control of the region and were referred to by the Celts as Germani, derived from the Celtic word meaning "the shouters"—possibly because of their loud war cries. The lands they conquered, present-day Germany, came to be called Germania. (In later centuries, the Germanic peoples also were known as the Teutons or Teutonic tribes.)

Roman Rule

Originally, the Germani thrived throughout the Middle Rhine region. Around 58 B.C., however, not long after the Celts were pushed out, the Romans consolidated their power in Gaul (France) and the "Romanization" of Europe—in which their culture influenced nearly every aspect of life—began.

Roman armies led by Julius Caesar went on to vanquish the Germani who lived in Gaul. This region became the northeastern frontier of the Roman Empire, and the

Rhine became the de facto border between Rome's territory and that of the Germani. The Roman legions then set up military camps at various strategic points along the Rhine, and over the years many villages and towns grew up within or around these strongholds.

The Romans were great engineers and constructed a series of aqueducts to carry the waters of the Rhine to distant villages. The Romans also built roads for military purposes. In 56 B.C., when Caesar wanted to extend Roman power over the tribes on the German side of the Rhine, he ordered construction of the first bridge across the river so that his legions could easily cross into enemy territory. Built between Koblenz and Andernach, this extraordinary feat of engineering, performed with only the most basic tools, was accomplished in only ten days. A second bridge was constructed farther upstream three years later.

By 50 B.C. the Romans had established forts on Lake Constance, and by 40 B.C. they had constructed garrisons

The Romans cross the Rhine River and enter Gaul in 58 B.C. The Rhine marked the border between Roman and Germani territory.

in present-day Cologne, Koblenz, Mainz, and elsewhere to protect the Rhine frontier from the Germani, who continued to occupy the territory on the east bank of the river. In the following years at least fifty more Roman forts were built along the Rhine.

The Romans' attempts to conquer the territory east of the Rhine largely came to naught. Moreover, they found the Germani more than willing to attack them. In 16 B.C. the Romans decided to take on the Germani in an all-out effort to conquer their land. After a series of battles and skirmishes, however, they were defeated in A.D. 9 and soon gave up their plan to conquer Germania. By A.D. 80 the Germani were pushing the Romans south again, back down the Rhine. To hold back the invaders, whom the Romans considered barbarians, the legions began construction on a line of forts connected by earthen and stone walls. This German line, or Limes Germanicus, connected with a similar structure that ran to the Danube. Together these lines of defense were more than 340 miles long with 37 miles running along the eastern bank of the Rhine.

This woodcut shows Roman soldiers attacking a German fortress during the Roman expansion into eastern Europe.

Barbarians Along the Rhine

In the early centuries A.D., *the German tribes who battled the Romans along the Rhine were referred to as barbarians, a term with negative connotations. But as Diether Etzel writes on the "Barbarians" website, the main crime committed by the barbarians was opposing the Roman invasion of their homeland along the Rhine:*

The term "Barbarian" is Greek in origin. The Greeks originally [applied it to] the peoples of Northern Europe because to them, the harsh "barking" sound of their speech sounded to them like "Bar-bar-bar." Since these strangers from the north did not understand classic Greek, the Greeks believed them to be "illiterate." The term also came to mean "stranger" or "wanderer," since most of the Barbarians with which they came in contact were nomadic....

Because most of these "strangers" regularly practiced raids upon [the Greek and Roman] civilizations, the term "Barbarian" gradually evolved into a pejorative term: a person who was sub-human, uncivilized, and regularly practiced the most vile and inhuman acts imaginable.... [But by besieging] the empire for 4 centuries, the Germans finally managed, during the 5th century A.D., to sack Rome and bring the once mighty empire to its knees....

It was, actually, Rome who drew "first blood" against the Germanic tribes. Rome wished to claim the lands north of the Rhine river for its own. Up to that point in time, the Germanic people had been content to "live and let live," with a few border skirmishes and forays. When Rome crossed the line and entered the Teutonic lands with intent to conquer, the Germanic tribesmen rose up in fury. After several failings, the Teutons managed to defeat the Roman invasion at the battle of Teutoberg Forest (circa A.D. 9) to such a great extent that Rome never again tried to conquer the Barbarian Germans.

In constant conflict with the Germani along the Rhine, the Romans used the river as a barrier to keep the enemy from invading their territory on the west bank. Goronwy Rees describes this phenomenon:

It was perhaps natural that the Romans should look on the Rhine as a frontier, a line of division, a means of defence; for Rome was essentially a road empire, whose communications ran by land and not by water. It was also a soldiers' empire, an empire of the legions, for whom a great river was a military obstacle, something to cross or to defend, not a route by which to travel.

Yet the Rhine frontier established by Rome was not yet a boundary between nations, because nations in the modern sense did not yet exist. It was a frontier between civilization and barbarism, between Roman law and tribal custom, and in time it was to become also a linguistic frontier.[8]

The Great Migration

With their soldiers, fortresses, and walls, the Romans maintained control of the Rhine, establishing several towns, such as Bonn, Cologne (Köln), and Trier, that would thrive throughout the centuries and grow into major cities. In some places these outposts were built to mimic the great city of Rome itself. The village of Trier, for example, was the site of an amphitheater that could seat twenty thousand spectators to watch bloody battles between gladiators and wild animals.

Yet the Rhine was not an impregnable barrier, and around the year 253 a group of Germanic tribes known as Franks, or Free Men, from the Main region began to conquer territory along the Lower and Middle Rhine that had been held by Rome for hundreds of years.

The Romans continued to battle the Franks and various Germanic tribes with varying success until 455, when the Franks finally prevailed and gained possession of the western bank of the Rhine. By 486 the Roman rule of more than four centuries had finally come to an end.

As the Romans were losing control of their empire, what is known as "the great migration" began. Tribes such as the Vandals, the Burgundians, the Visigoths, and the Alemanni came from North Africa and across Europe to settle throughout the valleys of the Rhine, with the Franks continuing to dominate the region.

The Frankish Kings

Under the Frankish king Clovis I, who ruled from 481 to 511, the power of the Franks grew considerably. As the powerful tribe subjugated the others in the region, the Frankish kingdom grew to include not only the Rhine but much of the European continent.

Clovis converted to Christianity in 496, and under his reign the king established close relations with the Roman church. During the next several centuries, the Christian religion spread throughout the Rhine region and came to dominate medieval Europe. Churches were constructed in former Roman settlements, and religious leaders were given great powers in villages and towns.

In 768 the Frankish king Charlemagne established his court in the Rhineland city of Aachen near Cologne.

King Clovis I (below) defeats the Alemmani in 496 (left).

Charlemagne died in 814, and his empire was partitioned into three sections by the Treaty of Verdun in 877. The Rhine acted as a dividing line between the East Frankish Kingdom, now Germany and Austria, and the West Frankish Kingdom, now France. This ancient division of land along the Rhine would remain controversial for centuries, and the French and the Germans would battle over control of the river periodically until World War II. The division had other consequences as well, Goronwy Rees writes:

> [In] the new Europe that was born in 887, the Rhine assumed a different significance from what it had had before. As Roman civilization decayed, it was slowly replaced by feudalism. But the new masters of Europe were not engineers like the Romans. They had neither the material resources nor the technical skill to maintain the magnificent Roman road system, and as the roads disintegrated they were replaced by rivers as a means of communication. The function of the Rhine as the natural frontier between France and Germany was taken over by [other rivers]...and the Rhine itself became a part of the new Europe's river network.
>
> Thus in the Middle Ages the Rhine fulfilled the same function as [commonly]...ascribed to it today.... "The Rhine is a Road!"[9]

Castles Along the Rhine

While kings and nobility divided up European territories, life for the average citizen was extremely difficult. In the centuries that followed the signing of the Treaty of Verdun, the region fractured into small feudal states in which all land was owned by wealthy nobles. In order to grow crops on small parcels of land, peasant farmers, called serfs, were forced to pay exorbitant fees in cash, crops, and livestock. Meanwhile, young men, called vassals, pledged themselves to perform military service for their lords in exchange for grants of land and privileges. Roger A. Toepfe describes the hardships of life as a serf:

> The pitiful plight of the serf was that he was bound to the land, and he was subject to the jurisdiction of an over-lord by virtue of his birth. The over-lord claimed the right of life or death over the serf. A peasant was not born into subjugation, but was a tenant of a parcel of land to be worked. As times became more difficult for the over-lord, the peasant suffered by paying greater and greater amounts of tithing and taxes. As a result, great despair spread among the peasantry.[10]

The feudal states in which serfs lived during the twelfth, thirteenth, and fourteenth centuries were numerous, each ruled by powerful knights from castles built high on the cliffs above the river. These castles were built by thousands of serfs who were forced to quarry stones from the riverbank and drag them up the extremely steep hills for use in construction.

A German castle rises high atop the foothills along the Rhine.

Knights built these castles for two reasons. One was that such locations were highly defensible, as would-be intruders could easily be repelled as they tried to scale the heights. With many well-armed and powerful figures inhabiting a small area, conflict was almost inevitable. Skirmishes between neighboring castles were common. As William Graves writes:

> Blood, in fact, runs through the history of the Rhine Gorge almost as plentiful as the Rhine itself. Along the world-famous chasm through the Taunus Mountains, scarcely a castle or ruin—Marksburg, Gutenfels, Sooneck, Reichenstein—tells a happy or peaceful story. Even those with quaint names, such as the fortress "Cat" . . . and "Mouse" memorialize the Rhine's dark past. . . .
>
> Lacking a powerful emperor or king, Teutonic knights fortified the heights along the narrow gorge and set themselves up as independent rulers.[11]

The commanding position of the castles also meant that those who owned them ruled the river, and they could stop ships by stretching chains and ropes across the waterway, allowing only those who paid a toll to pass. The thirty-five-mile stretch of the Rhine Gorge between Bingen and Koblenz was ideal for this purpose, and for this reason the area was home to more castles than anywhere else in the world. According to William Graves: "For income between wars, they turned to the historic river trade, levying tolls on all ships that passed."[12]

Merchants Take Control

The Rhine knights did not rule the river unopposed, however. Almost as soon as the first castles were built, groups of traders organized themselves in attempts to keep the river open. In 1254, for example, the League of Rhenish Cities was established by the bishoprics of three Rhine cities, Mainz, Cologne, and Trier. The objective of the League—only partially fulfilled—was to rid the Rhine of the so-called robber-knights and allow free travel and trade along the river. Also, at least briefly, a more powerful nation-builder imposed some order on the region. Rudolph of Hapsburg, the king of Germany, came to power in the 1270s and raised a powerful army that pillaged and destroyed several castles, including Rheinstein, Reichenstein, and Rheinecke.

Political confusion reigned along the Rhine throughout the next several centuries as weak royalty failed to unite the various interests along the river. As various local rulers fought among themselves for power, groups of merchants in larger cities, such as Strasbourg and Cologne, banded together to form strong, local governments and declared independence from any outside rulers.

A Watery Dividing Line

In the Middle Ages, the Rhine was the dividing line between two very distinct European cultures, the Romanized French and the Teutonic Germans. While the French were Christians who followed ancient law and culture as developed by the Romans, the Germans were called pagans because they rejected Christianity. Goronwy Rees explains in The Rhine:

To all the other reasons which prevented the growth of a strong national state in the Rhine basin, one further one must be added. The Rhine was not only the frontier between Romans and Teutons, between law and custom, between civilization and barbarism; it also became the frontier between Christianity and paganism, and the boundary across which, and the road by which, the Church tried to extend its spiritual domain. Missionary efforts to the Germans were concentrated in the three bishoprics immediately west of the Rhine-Cologne, Trier and Mainz. The missionaries sailed up the Rhine to convert the Saxons and Friesians of the northern plain; from Trier, by way of Moselle, they made their way to Coblenz and up the Lahn; Mainz especially had a particularly wide ecclesiastical jurisdiction, and from there the Gospel spread north, east and south along the Main and the Necker and...the Alps and Bohemia.

Many of these wealthy German towns, in turn, joined together to form a large trade organization called the Hanseatic League, which oversaw shipping and trade from London to Russia and Norway.

A Plague Along the River

By enabling the peoples of central Europe to trade with one another, the Rhine served as a source of wealth in the region. But it also brought extreme suffering and death. In the middle of the fourteenth century a disaster more deadly than the robber-knights swept along the Rhine Valley. The bubonic plague, or Black Death, which had first erupted in the Gobi Desert in Central Asia in 1320, hit western Europe around 1347.

Although it was not understood at the time, the bacterial disease was carried by fleas that lived on black rats that infested the holds of ships carrying trade goods

Parishioners bear the corpse of a victim of the bubonic plague in this eighteenth-century painting.

between Europe and Asia. When infected fleas bit humans, victims became gravely ill as internal bleeding caused dark purple discoloration of the skin. The disease was nearly 100 percent fatal, and victims died within days. By the time the epidemic abated, an estimated 18 to 35 million people in Europe had died out of a total of about 72 million.

The Black Plague followed the Rhine trade route in 1348 and swept into Switzerland, Germany, and France. The plague claimed other victims who were not even infected, however. In the climate of fear and ignorance of the time, people looked for someone to blame—and Jews were falsely accused of spreading the disease. On the "Jewish History Sourcebook: The Black Death and the Jews 1348–1349 CE" Web page, historian Paul Halsall describes how this led to the deaths of thousands of Jewish people in the Rhine Valley:

The figure of Black Death draws its bow in this rendition of the horrendous epoch of the Black Plague.

> By authority of Amadeus VI, Count of Savoy, a number of the Jews who lived [in Switzerland], having been arrested and put to the torture, naturally confessed anything their inquisitors suggested. These Jews, under torture, incriminated others. Records of their confessions were sent from one town to another in Switzerland and down the Rhine River into Germany, and as a result, thousands of Jews, in at least two hundred towns and hamlets, were butchered and burnt.[13]

Naturally, such a massacre did not stop the plague, which continued to sweep across Europe for the next 250 years. Ironically, the plague and accompanying anarchy and hysteria helped loosen the grip of feudalism in Europe, leading to increased freedom for the surviving peasants. The massive die-off created a labor shortage, and those who survived found that they could demand better treatment from the nobility who owned the land or higher wages by hiring themselves out as freemen in towns or other manors.

Conflict in the Rhineland

The death of feudalism may have provided people living along the Rhine a measure of freedom, but life was still hard, as frequent wars visited destruction on towns, and peasants found themselves conscripted into the armies of their local rulers. One particularly devastating conflict raged from 1618 to 1648. Known as the Thirty Years' War, this conflagration's effect on the Rhine Valley is described by Walther Ottendorf-Simrock in *Castles on the Rhine*:

> The Thirty Years' War, which raged intermittently all over Germany... involved France, Spain and Sweden in an indecisive struggle of Catholic [France and Spain] versus Protestant [Sweden and Germany] states. Soldiers from all over Europe—imperial troops, soldiers of the Catholic "League" and the Protestant "Union," Frenchman, Spaniards, Swedes—all struggled for supremacy in the Rhine Valley, and the castles, strategical key-positions in the seventeenth century no less than when they were built, changed hands repeatedly.[14]

Even after the Thirty Years' War came to an indecisive end, the Rhine area continued to be the site of death and destruction, as France sponsored raids on the region for the next five decades in an effort to keep Germany weak. French troops destroyed many towns, villages, castles, and even individual farms. The French also occupied some territory for decades at a time; for example, by taking the Alsace region, they controlled the west side of the Rhine from the city of Basel north to Speyer. Control of some cities, such as Mainz, bounced back and forth with the French occupying it in 1792, losing it to Germany in 1793, and taking it again in 1797 and holding it until 1815.

Conflict continued almost unabated as the armies of French emperor Napoléon Bonaparte marched across Europe between 1798 and 1812. In 1806 Napoléon incorporated Bavaria, Baden, and other German and Swiss principalities into a league of states known as the Confederation of the Rhine, which made up the western border of the league. After Napoléon's final defeat in 1812 the confederation was dissolved.

Napoléon (center) at Waterloo. Napoléon established the Confederation of the Rhine in 1806.

In 1815 the Congress of Vienna was formed to reestablish the borders of the European countries after changes made by Napoléon. In Germany the state of Prussia was expanded to include the Rhineland from the Moselle region all the way north to the Netherlands. At this time France retained the Alsace region while the independent states of Germany, such as Prussia, were grouped into a nation known as the German Confederation, or Deutsches Bund.

Over the next half century, the Prussian state rose to dominate Europe as it unified the various German states into the German Empire, or Deutsches Reich. Prussian chancellor Otto von Bismarck maintained that Alsace rightly belonged to the German Empire and in 1870 attacked France to reclaim the region. The Franco-German War ended quickly with Germany defeating France. After the war the west bank of the Rhine was once again part of Germany, with the Alsace and Lorraine regions incorporated into the German Empire.

The World Wars

A thirst for revenge grew in France over the forfeiture of Alsace-Lorraine until 1914, when World War I broke out. Once again, German soldiers stormed across the Rhine as they had done in 1870, expecting a quick victory. Instead they got bogged down for four years of senseless, destructive warfare, as the French were joined by England, the United States, and Russia to defeat the Germans. After millions died, little had changed but that Alsace-Lorraine was returned to France.

As the French counted their dead, they vowed that they would never again let the Germans invade their country from across the Rhine. To protect their country from what they called the "beast that sleeps on the other side of the Rhine,"[15] the French decided to imitate the first-century Romans and build their own Limes Germanicus. Between 1929 and 1940 the French spent millions of dollars to construct the Maginot line, a 150-mile-long fortified network of heavily armed forts and underground bunkers that paralleled France's eastern border with Germany.

Nothing the French did could protect them when a former corporal in the German army, Adolf Hitler, seized the reigns of power in Germany in 1933. Once again the Rhine figured prominently, as Hitler, in speeches and printed propaganda, contended that the Rhine was not part of the border between Germany and France, but an important part of Germany—along with the Alsace-Lorraine region to the west of the Rhine.

By the late 1930s Hitler's troops were militarizing the Rhine along their own version of the Maginot line, called the Siegfried line, built on the German bank from the Swiss border to near Karlsruhe between 1936 and 1939, the year World War II began. In 1940 the Germans bypassed the Maginot line and conquered France in a matter of days.

Adolf Hitler, flanked by Nazi officers, poses before the Eiffel Tower in June 1940.

Bombs Along the Rhine

Over the years the Rhine had become home to much of German industry with chemical plants, pharmaceutical factories, and steel mills lining the banks of the river. During World War II this region was bombed relentlessly by the United States and the other Allies. The industrial areas in the Ruhr region, where the Nazis manufactured their tanks, airplanes, and other military hardware, were flattened. Roads, railways, power plants, docks, canals, and power lines were destroyed while cities, towns, and villages were reduced to rubble. Priceless works of centuries-old art and architecture were destroyed, and millions of people on all sides of the conflict were killed.

But the Rhine remained, as always, a formidable barrier. After the Allies invaded Normandy in France in June 1944, they were soon able to win from Nazi forces the west bank of the Rhine from Switzerland to the North Sea. But from the Netherlands to Switzerland, as the Germans retreated, Hitler ordered his troops to blow up every bridge left standing across the Rhine so that the Allied soldiers would not be able to follow with their heavy equipment. This strategy forced the war to drag on for another year, as Goronwy Rees explains:

Allied troops cross the Remagen Bridge on March 11, 1945.

An Old Bridge Falls to War

During times of war, bridges are viewed as extremely important structures for allowing the movement of men and equipment across rivers. During World War II many bridges across the Rhine were destroyed, either by the Allies hoping to slow the Germans or by the Nazis as a way of stopping the advance of Allied armies. In the April 1967 article in National Geographic, *"The Rhine: Europe's River of Legend," William Graves describes the story of one bridge at Remagen that still had not been rebuilt when the article was written more than twenty years after the war ended:*

Beside the river south of Bonn stand three massive stone towers amid a jumble of masonry—all that remains of the bridge at Remagen.

On the morning of March 7, 1945, units of the American First Army, seeking a break in Rhine defenses, found the bridge intact. German engineers, with grim efficiency, had blown [up] all other heavy spans across the river; Remagen's turn was to come at four o'clock that afternoon. But Remagen's turn never came.

Minutes before [German demolition teams were to set off their explosives], American infantry and engineers raced across the bridge under fire and cut the electric cables leading to the demolition charges. The bridge, an old one, held up long enough for armor and more infantry to cross. Ten days later it collapsed [from the weight of the heavy machinery], never to be rebuilt. The break-through at Remagen smashed a gap in Hitler's [defensive] West Wall and hastened the final chapter of the war.

[After] the Allied invasion of Normandy...the Rhine became a formidable barrier to the Allied advance. Failure to seize a bridgehead across the river in 1944 meant that the war was prolonged into 1945, through long months of immeasurable suffering and destruction, even though Germany's armies in the west were routed and disorganized. Behind the barrier of the Rhine, they were able to reform and refit with consequences which were to be of momentous historical importance to Europe.

During those months, the Allies continued their immensely destructive air bombardment of Germany, in which the Rhine and its cities suffered appalling damage. In that terrible air offensive, many of the Rhine's greatest treasures were lost.[16]

Only one bridge, a 1,069-foot railroad bridge at Remagen, remained standing across the Rhine, and in March 1945 the Allies were finally able to seize it and get enough troops across the river to pursue the fleeing Nazis and end the war.

A New Era of Stability

After World War II the Middle Rhine once again became the borderline between France and Germany. The industrial and agricultural power of the Rhine Valley was slowly rebuilt, and by the 1960s factories along the Rhine were once again producing steel and chemicals, as well as some of the highest quality consumer goods in the world. The surprising German recovery in so short a time after World War II was referred to as an "economic miracle."

By the first years of the twenty-first century, calm had reigned along the banks of the Rhine for nearly six decades—possibly longer than at any time during the previous two thousand years. With the Rhine River at the center of a powerful economic confederation known as the European Union, its waters are busier than ever. The Rhine plays a vital role in tourism, transportation, agriculture, industry, and in its more scenic stretches, simply lifting the spirits of those who gaze upon it. After centuries of conflict the Rhine continues to flow and serve as the lifeblood of the now peaceful heart of Europe.

3

A River of Commerce and Industry

The Rhine has been a rich resource for humans since they first settled along its banks in prehistoric times. In addition to serving as a frontier, the river has been a vital part of the region's economy—key to commerce, industry, agriculture, and travel. Sometimes these varied interests comfortably coincide; sometimes they clash.

The first use of the Rhine was for transportation. Around three thousand years ago the Celts skillfully plied the river waters in high-sided wooden boats powered by leather sails. In later years, the river served primarily as an important military supply route for the Roman legions that occupied the banks of the Rhine. The legions used boats to travel and move troops between the many forts on the Limes Germanicus. During this time the first boat-building centers were established at Cologne and Mainz to serve the Roman military and also local commercial interests.

Some of the most important items the Roman merchants shipped via the Rhine were lumber from the Black Forest, locally caught fish, and salt used to make a particularly popular fish sauce. The Romans also moved

This woodcut shows the old city of Cologne, among the first significant military and commercial ports along the Rhine.

quarried stone along the river—building blocks for their fortresses and defensive walls. These goods were transported on flat rafts or in boats similar to large canoes, rowed by two men.

Shipping on the Rhine

With the fall of the Roman Empire, trade along the Rhine greatly diminished. For centuries the river waters remained relatively deserted except for local fishermen. By the Middle Ages, however, the Rhine was becoming one of the busiest shipping lanes in Europe. As a major north-south artery, the river proved invaluable to those wanting to move goods from the North Sea into the land-locked heart of Europe. Products such as grain, fur, timber, honey, fish, salt, coal, flax cloth, and handcrafted goods such as cookware, tools, furniture, and weapons moved up and down the river. Boats plied the Rhine waters from distant cities in England, Scandinavia, Russia, and elsewhere. During this time, goods were moved mainly by rowboats and sailboats. In some places where the river-banks were wide enough, towpaths were built along the river, and flatboats moving against the current were pulled along by oxen, horses, or even people. There was also a

Special Boats for a Special River

In earlier centuries, ships could not sail from one end of the Rhine to the other because of natural barriers such as rocks, sandbanks, shallows, and eddies. To aid shipping, special vessels were built to traverse different parts of the river, as Monka I. Baumgarten writes in Baedeker's Rhine:

On the Upper and Middle Rhine the shallowness of the river and the narrowness of the channel at certain points made it necessary to use vessels of shallow draught, and the main traffic [moved] downstream. A variety of types were developed: on the Upper Rhine the "Lauertanne" [a canoelike boat used for a single trip downstream then broken up into usable lumber] and the "Schnieke" [similar to the "Lauertanne" but mainly used by the shipowners of Strasbourg], on the Middle Rhine the "Oberländer"

[a square-shaped boat used around Cologne] and the "Schelch" [a flat-bottomed boat used around Mainz]....
The principal type was the "Aak" [a barge-like vessel with built-in living quarters], which...remained in use for centuries.

Towards the end of the 18th century shipping and trading relationships between the Upper and Lower Rhine intensified. As a result the types of vessel used were to a considerable extent unified, with Dutch influences remaining predominant.

The 19th century brought revolutionary changes to shipping on the Rhine. The first steamship to sail on the river, in 1816, was the British-built "Prince of Orange", which left Rotterdam on 8 June, reached Cologne on the 12th and from there was towed upstream to Koblenz by horses.

Merchants ply the Rhine in specially designed boats. At right, a boatman commandeers a common cargo vessel.

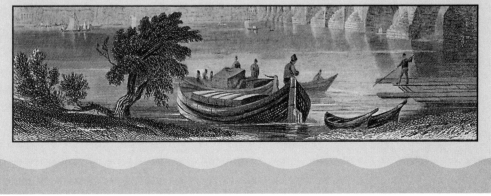

profusion of small "market boats," so called because they carried locally grown produce between towns.

In addition to moving products, the Rhine was a major transportation artery, as Roy E. Mellor writes in *The Rhine: A Study in the Geography of Water Transport:*

> River boats were also widely used for passenger transport. A notable traffic was [religious] pilgrims, especially on the Upper Rhine going to [the Lady Chapel in] Einsiedeln, [Switzerland].... There are also records of delegates going to major church conferences or political meetings using the river: for example, on 4th December 1446, the *Bürgermeister* [mayor] of Basel and his party left by boat for a peace conference at Münster in Westphalia, reaching Köln on [the] 13th December.... Many princes along the Rhine had their own yachts for making their official journeys.[17]

The invention of the steamship in the late eighteenth century dramatically changed the way people and products moved along the Rhine. These coal-powered ships shortened the length of an eight-day trip between Rotterdam and Cologne to only four days.

By 1824 regular steamship service was established on the Rhine with various cities investing in their own shipping lines. For example, the city fathers of Cologne established the Prussian Rhine Steamship Company in 1826. The business was one of the first stock companies in Germany, and the shareholders were nearly all of the people who lived in Cologne. As steamships became more powerful and river hazards were cleared away, longer stretches of the Rhine became navigable, and trips that once took days were reduced to hours. Meanwhile, companies that built steamships set up shop along the riverbanks in the Netherlands and Germany.

Great improvements in ship design and construction radically changed shipping on the Rhine as the nineteenth century progressed. Powerful tugboats were first invented

Transporting cattle along the Rhine in 1865. Steamships like this one were in wide use among Rhine-area stock companies by the mid-1800s.

in the 1820s and steadily improved in the following decades, until one tugboat could be used to tow from four to six barges at once, moving up to 220,000 pounds of goods at a time. This development meant that products could be shipped more efficiently, making them cheaper and more widely available to the average citizen.

In the 1840s the first iron barges were constructed. By the end of the century these huge cargo transporters had doubled in size while their capacity increased tenfold. By the 1910s gas- and diesel-powered tugs and self-propelled barges replaced the steam engines that had so altered shipping in the nineteenth century.

Meanwhile, passenger steamships were put into service, offering comfortable and affordable travel to average citizens. By the late nineteenth century these steamers were virtually floating hotels, offering sumptuous meals, musical and theatrical entertainment, and plush accommodations.

Rhine Shipping Today

Heavy bombing by the Allies during World War II caused the near total destruction of shipping on the Rhine. Harbors were destroyed, the remains of fallen bridges blocked the river, unexploded bombs lay on the river bottom, and burned-out hulks of sunken ships were scattered everywhere.

In the decades after the war, however, shipping was revived, thanks to the cooperation of countries that were former enemies. While the Allied powers helped Germany clear the wreckage from the Rhine, other countries invested heavily in river projects. The Dutch, for example, led the way on new harbor construction at the Rotterdam-Europort facilities. The French rebuilt the ports of Strasbourg in the Alsace-Lorraine region, while the "economic miracle" of postwar West Germany allowed a rebuilding of its industrial base along the Rhine.

The new fleets of ships consisted mainly of self-propelled barges, known as the "Rhine-Herne" or "Europa barge," that were capable of moving up to nearly fifteen hundred tons. When the push tug (as opposed to tugs that pulled) came into use in the 1950s, even larger quantities of goods, especially coal and steel, began to move up and down the river.

Push tugs, with extremely powerful engines, are able to move barges that are tightly lashed together and can carry up to sixteen thousand tons. With the pushing movement, these huge loads are easier to steer and maneuver through tight spaces, such as under bridges and into harbors. In addition, smaller crews are needed because, unlike a line of barges being pulled, barges pushed in this manner do not need sailors to steer them. This also gives the barges more room for carrying cargo, since onboard crew accommodations such as bunkhouses and cabins are unnecessary. And in the 1960s and 1970s, improvements in radar and closed-circuit television enabled tugboat captains to work at night and in fog and other inclement weather.

Goods transported on Rhine ships and barges vary widely, but the bulk of the freight consists of the raw materials used by Europe's heavy industries. The most common items are oil, oil products, and iron ore, which make up about 37 percent of all commercial products shipped along the river. Mineral building products, mostly sand and gravel taken from quarries near the river, along with cement from processing plants, compose another 30 percent of shipping traffic. Coal, which once dominated the shipping scene, has fallen to less than 8 percent as factories become more efficient and require less of the polluting fuel. Ships moving these materials are joined by those transporting a wide variety of sometimes toxic or hazardous substances such as fertilizers, pesticides, industrial chemicals, metallic waste, and other toxic by-products of manufacturing. These goods compose about 6 percent of the total. Foodstuffs such as grain, animal fodder, edible oils, salt, and other products account for just 9 percent of the traffic.

The Industrial Rhine

From the time the first brickworks were built along the Rhine more than two thousand years ago, the river has been a site where industry has coexisted with agriculture. By the end of the eighteenth century, the shores of the Rhine had become home to paper mills, dye and textile factories, tanneries, steel mills, and chemical plants.

The heart of European industry is Germany's Rhine-Ruhr district, where one of the largest reserves of bituminous coal in western Europe is found. In addition to its importance as fuel, coal is a basic material in many products manufactured in the region. For example, coal is used to make certain dyes, and by the nineteenth century, the Rhine-based German dye industry was one of the most important in the world. In 1863 German businessman Friedrich Bayer opened a coal-tar dye plant along the banks of the Rhine. By 1897 scientists had discovered ways to use coal tar in aspirin, and by the twentieth

The Rotterdam Europort

The Europort in Rotterdam, opened in 1966, is the busiest port in the world. Every year over thirty-one thousand ships use the port to handle, among other products, more than 104 million tons of crude oil, 22 million tons of refined oil, 30 million tons of iron ore, and 23 million tons of coal. The facilities are described on the PortofRotterdam.com website:

Rotterdam is one of the world's most important junctions when it comes to cargo traffic. Every year, over 300 million [tons] of goods are handled here. Located on the North Sea—the busiest sea route in the world—this Dutch port serves a European [continent] of about 380 million consumers....

The port of Rotterdam covers an area of [about twenty-five miles], from the center of the city to the North Sea. The port and industrial area covers... 26,000 acres. Around 30,000 seagoing vessels and 130,000 inland vessels arrive in the port every year. Rotterdam is the home port...for around 500 shipping lines that maintain regular services to 1,000 ports. Rotterdam is Europe's most important port for oil & chemicals, containers, iron ore, coal, food and metals....

Goods bound for the [European continent] can leave the port by river, rail, road, pipeline or sea. For large quantities of bulk goods, transport via the Rhine, which flows into the sea at Rotterdam, is ideal....

Characteristic of a mainport like Rotterdam is that all kinds of different goods flows come together. These various types of goods, such as oil, ores and coal, or fruit and dry bulk, roll-on/roll-off and containers are usually handled by specialized companies. These companies are established in specific parts of the port, so that Rotterdam is characterized by a collection of specialized ports [for oil, foodstuffs, and other items].

century, the Bayer Company was one of the biggest aspirin makers in the world.

The abundant coal deposits in the Ruhr region also attracted one of the largest concentrations of steel and iron production in the world. The twenty-four-hundred-square-mile Rhine-Ruhr area was transformed from a sleepy agricultural district to an industrial powerhouse in the mid-nineteenth century after the first coal mines were opened in the region. By the beginning of the twentieth century, riverbanks in this area were lined with foundries, blast furnaces, and rolling mills that produced huge rolls of flat steel. These factories belched smoke, heat, and chemical fumes as red-hot iron was converted to steel, which was poured and shaped within their walls.

Cities expanded up and down the Rhine as demand for German products grew, each region specializing in specific industries. For example, Essen is famous for steel mills, while factories in Bochum focus on producing tin, zinc, and iron that is used in a wide variety of consumer goods from automobiles to electric lamps. Dortmund is home to manufacturers of wire cable, mining machinery, and railroad tracks, and Gelsenkirchen concentrates on production of petrochemical derivatives such as fertilizers, solvents, pharmaceuticals, and pesticides. Duisburg is noted for its steel mills as well as its port facilities.

One stretch of the river, where the Rhine is joined by the Ruhr, is particularly heavily industrialized. The beginning of this segment is abrupt, prompting an unflattering description from one observer in the 1960s:

> Nothing prepares a passenger on the Rhine for his first view of Germany's industrial heart, the Ruhr. At a turn in the river it simply erupts from the green landscape like a volcanic island thrust from the sea. The towering shapes of blast furnaces and smoke-blackened chimneys gives the impression of so many giant cinder cones....
>
> [The] Ruhr is one continuous factory, forever wrapped in dark clouds of its own breath. Night transforms the Ruhr into a gigantic blowtorch, searing both the sky above and, by reflection, the Rhine below.[18]

More recently, however, the number of steel mills has declined along the Rhine. Competition from steel produced more cheaply in other countries caused many

German facilities to shut down in the 1970s. These were replaced by electronics and computer manufacturers in addition to producers of industrial chemicals. Still, manufacturing is the mainstay of the Rhine-Ruhr region and over 4 million people earn a living there in a variety of industries.

Wine Along the Rhine

While the Rhine is well known for its importance to industry and transportation, it is also famous for the wine produced from grapes grown on hillsides that rise above the river. Just how long people along the Rhine have been making wine is uncertain. It is believed that grapevines have been planted throughout the region north of the Alps since prehistoric times, and the Celts may have drunk grape juice that had fermented into wine. The art of winemaking, however, did not exist along the Rhine until the Romans brought it to the Alsace and Moselle regions in the first century B.C. As Stuart Pigott writes:

This painting shows a Roman horseman sounding a horn in the Alsace region of northeastern France.

[The] Romans planted vines in the cool river valleys of northwestern Germany. They knew that the hill country there was too inhospitable for wine-growing, however. . . . This led them to sheltered pockets in the steep-sided river valleys that cut deep into the hills. By the fourth century AD, they had planted significant areas of vineyards in many of the sites that continue to be regarded as Germany's top vineyards.[19]

After the fall of the Roman Empire, winemaking continued, carried on by communities of monks and by vintners employed by the region's princes, nobles, and kings. Over the centuries, wine from the Rhineland evolved a distinctive flavor and character that sets it apart from wines made elsewhere. As Stuart Pigott writes: "Today's wines are the result of centuries of experimentation begun by the Romans, continued by monks throughout the Middle Ages and Renaissance, and carried to fruition by the aristocracy and landed gentry during the 19th century."[20]

In pursuit of the perfect wine, grapes were planted along vast stretches of the Rhine and on the slopes overlooking its many tributaries. Because growing conditions along these various waterways vary considerably, the characteristics of the grapes and wines they produce vary as well. The wines are, therefore, grouped according to the general areas from which they come.

Today Rhineland wine regions include Baden, which reaches from Switzerland to Mannheim on the east bank of the river; Pfalz, on the west bank slopes of the Haardt Mountains between Karlsruhe and Worms; Rheinhessen, on the west between Worms and Mainz around the Neirstein River; Mittelrhein, under the cliff-top castles between Bingen and Bonn; Rheingau, a small area under the Taunus Mountains around Wiesbaden north of Mainz; and Moselle, which covers the entire Moselle River region down to its confluence with the Rhine.

As varied as the grapes from the Rhineland may be, they are virtually all green and produce sweeter white wine varieties such as Riesling and Tokay d'Alsace. Because the purple grapes that produce red wines do not thrive in the cool Rhineland climate, white wines also predominate in the Alsace region of France south of Strasbourg and around Colmar. Instead of sweet, heavy wine, however, this region is known for its light, sparkling wines.

Throughout the Rhineland the steep, rocky terrain means that picking the grapes is an arduous process. Most vineyards still are harvested by the ancient method—by hand—with workers perched on narrow terraces filling large baskets with grapes. To select only the

French winemakers harvest grapes near Colmar, France, in 1950. Traditional winemaking techniques are still used throughout the Rhineland today.

The Ice Saints of Wine

The tradition of winemaking along the Rhine is marked by many centuries-old festivals celebrating planting and harvesting seasons. Each October in Mainz, for instance, Rhinelanders celebrate the grape harvest with Weinfesten, or "wine feasts," marked by the coronation of a Wine Queen. In Koblenz, spring is a time for a visit from three saints, Mamertus, Pancratius, and Servatius. In National Geographic William Graves explains their importance to the wine harvest:

Each spring the holy trio visits Germany's wine region and brings either a blessing or bad luck to the vineyards. Rhinelanders call them *die Eisheiligen*—the Ice Saints—and look forward with mixed feelings to the visit.

The Ice Saints arrive in spirit on May 11, 12, and 13, the individual feast days named for them in the church calendar. Tradition holds that the weather they bring with them—warm sunshine, or a sudden cold snap—foretells the size of the coming harvest in October.

Actually there is more than mere superstition to the Ice Saints, for along the Rhine and its sister stream, the Moselle, early May is a critical time for the young grapevines. Sudden spring frost can destroy the weaker vines at a moment when it is too late to replace them. The stronger vines generally escape without damage, but the total harvest is reduced.

finest grapes and leave behind poor-quality fruit, harvesters must climb up and down extremely steep hills, sweating in the summer and freezing in the fall.

The Rhine region also produces a fine brandy, Weinbrand, a high-alcohol drink distilled from wine. Large brandy distilleries in Mainz and the Rheingau region produce top-quality brandies that are aged for many years in wooden casks made from Black Forest timber. This brandy is typically drunk with water by local Rhinelanders.

In addition to grapes, the Rhineland farmers grow grains, potatoes, and beets along with dairy products, beef, pork, chicken, and eggs. Farther to the north, along the various branches of the Rhine in the Netherlands, farming is the mainstay of the economy. In the low-lying fields, cows, goats, and sheep may be seen grazing passively, their milk used for dozens of varieties of Dutch cheese and other dairy products.

Fun for Tourists

While industry and agriculture continue to be the basis for the Rhineland economy, from the 1970s on, tourism has been an increasingly important source of income.

Because most of the Rhine has been navigable throughout its history, travelers are not a new phenomenon. In the Middle Ages large groups of Christian pilgrims traveled down the river on their way to religious sites in Switzerland and Rome or as part of a much longer journey to the Holy Land. In the nineteenth century, the spa at Baden-Baden became a fashionable spot for people suffering from arthritis and respiratory problems.

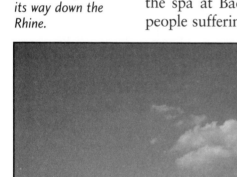

A cruise ship makes its way down the Rhine.

Today the Rhine River between Rotterdam and the Alps offers recreational pursuits to hikers, swimmers, boaters, bikers, and others.

Thanks to modern transportation networks, today nearly 75 million people live within a day's drive of the Rhine River, and the number of people spending their weekends and vacations in the Rhineland has grown considerably over the years. In addition, tourists from the United States, Great Britain, and Eastern Europe travel to the region to explore the Black Forest, the Alps, and the castles along the Rhine Gorge.

One of the most popular and relaxing tourist activities is cruising the Rhine by boat. Dozens of vessels deliver tourists to the most scenic regions of the river, with Lorelei Rock and the castles of the Rhine Gorge the most popular destinations. Tourists can elect one-day excursions or an extended cruise from Amsterdam to Basel on luxury boats. Well-heeled visitors may pay thousands of dollars for the five days of dining, dancing, and sightseeing that such cruises entail.

Visiting Castles Along the Rhine

Tour boats stop at many of the castles of the Rhine Gorge, which are extremely popular destinations for both foreign visitors and Germans. While many castles lie in ruins, their stone walls slowly crumbling into dust, others are well preserved or have been painstakingly restored. Only one, Marksburg, has remained completely intact since it was built around 1100. This castle has dominated the towering hill above Braubach for more than nine centuries and has survived nearly one thousand years of war, political upheaval, and civilization. Like a snapshot of ancient history, Marksburg holds a commanding view of the east bank of the Rhine and has changed little since Baron von Eppstein lived there in 1231. The 130-foot tower can be seen for miles, and the interior of the castle features ancient furnishings and dozens of suits of armor worn by medieval knights when they battled for supremacy along the banks of the Rhine. Inhabitants of the castles were some of the first people to collect tolls along the Rhine, and the river produced revenue for the robber-knights who lived there for centuries.

Marksburg was turned over to the Association for the Preservation of German Castles in 1899, which appropriately makes its headquarters in the building. Although the castle was damaged by Allied shelling near the end of World War II, it has been restored to near original condition since that time.

Castles such as Marksburg afford tourists many recreational activities including hiking the castle grounds, picnicking below the towering walls, or having coffee and snacks in the courtyards. And some castles, such as the Rheinfels near St. Goar and Lorelei Rock, have been restored for use as hotels. For several hundred dollars a night, tourists are able to sleep in royal splendor while enjoying the castle's commanding view of the Rhine.

Small towns along the river, such as St. Goar, also offer a wide variety of entertainment for the tourist. Restaurants feature world-renowned, traditional German beers and sausages while shops sell gifts such as cuckoo clocks, chocolates, and decorated beer steins.

Festivals Along the Rhine

For tourists along the Rhine much of their activity focuses on annual carnivals and festivals marked by parades, floats, costumes, eating, drinking, and singing. Some festivals are strictly local affairs, while others have a broader significance. The celebration of Fastnacht, for example, marks the beginning of Lent. The counterpart of the Mardi Gras carnival in the United States, Fastnacht, or "Fasting Eve," is recognition that a devout Catholic will have to enter a period of forty days of fasting and self-denial. Before this arrives, however, people celebrate with a final indulgence of food, drink, dancing, costume balls, and parades.

Another popular event is known as the "Rhine in Flames." This happens at various times in the summer

Fireworks light the sky during the Rhine in Flames *festival in St. Goar, Germany.*

when towns and villages along the river coordinate fireworks displays from strategic places. At dusk colorful explosions of light highlight castles, gorges, hilltops, forests, and fortresses. Spectators line the shores for the light show while the river is thick with private boats and cruise ships.

Hundreds of other festivals are held along the Rhine, many dedicated to art or music. One site that attracts a younger crowd is the Loreley Open Air Stage, a concert venue above Lorelei Rock with a breathtaking view of the Rhine Valley. This concert site features bands, dance and music festivals, art shows, and other cultural events throughout the warm months of spring and summer.

The time span represented by rock concerts and ancient castles is a reflection of the wide spectrum of attractions offered by the Rhine. High in the Swiss Alps, hikers may view the headwaters of the river while 820 miles away the bustling city of Rotterdam offers tourists museums, restaurants, and other cultural entertainment.

With its mix of agriculture, industry, shipping, and tourism, the Rhine provides millions of people with jobs and helps place Germany, France, Luxembourg, and the Netherlands among the richest countries in the world. As a river of commerce and industry, the Rhine has few rivals among the world's waterways.

4

· · · · · · · · · ·

A Struggling River

While the Rhine and its surrounding territory have been the site of human settlement for millennia, in the past 150 years parts of the river have been altered beyond recognition, largely as a result of human activities since the Industrial Revolution. Many of these changes have negatively affected the Rhine, along with the plants and animals that depend on the river for survival.

The most dramatic changes along the Rhine are the result of industrial development along the riverbanks, the massive dumping of industrial waste, and alterations in the river's natural flow due to the construction of canals, dams, and concrete channels. These transformations have caused the disappearance of 90 percent of the seven to eight hundred species of plants and animals that were once found in and along the river. Of the fifty original species of fish, only about a dozen survive.

Changes along the Rhine have also noticeably altered or destroyed the woodlands, wetlands, and meadows along the river's banks. While some 30 percent of the Alpine stretches of the river remain pristine, only 5 percent of the Middle Rhine has been left untouched. Along

An Ode to Sewage

English poet Samuel Taylor Coleridge.

The stench of pollution along the Rhine is nothing new. Until the twentieth century, cities did not have sewage systems and people used chamber pots for toilets. These were simply emptied out the windows every morning—or dumped into the local river. In 1814 renowned English poet Samuel Taylor Coleridge wrote "Cologne," a humorous ode to the smell of the Rhine, as he traveled through that city. It is reprinted in The Light in Holland by Anthony Bailey:

In Köhln [Cologne], a town of
   monks and bones,
And pavements fang'd with murder-
   ous stones,
And rags, and hags, and hideous
   wenches;
I counted two and seventy stenches,
All well defined, and several stinks!

Ye Nymphs that reign o'er sewers
   and sinks,
The River Rhine, it is well known,
Doth wash your city of Cologne;
But tell me, Nymphs, what power
   divine
Shall henceforth wash the River
   Rhine?

the Lower Rhine, less than 0.5 percent of the natural landscape has been preserved.

Taming the Rhine

Perhaps it is not surprising that fish were among the first species to be negatively affected by human activity on the Rhine. Until the mid-nineteenth century, the waters of the river flashed a dazzling silver from the half million Atlantic salmon that migrated upstream from the sea to the gravelly beds of the Lower Rhine and its tributaries to spawn. But even at that time, the salmon were struggling to survive as their natural habitat was altered by dredging and dams. By 1885 the problem was so severe that the nations along the Rhine signed the Salmon Treaty, setting up the International Salmon Commission to protect the fish.

Despite the commission's efforts, by the beginning of the twentieth century the salmon had nearly disappeared from the Rhine. Overfishing had depleted their numbers, but the greatest damage was caused by the channeling and straightening of the river: The problem was that salmon swim out to sea when they are eighteen months old but return to where they hatched to spawn three or four years later. The construction of dams along the

A 1905 painting depicts the Rhine as it may have appeared in centuries past.

Rhine prevented the salmon from returning to their spawning grounds, and the fish that had lived in the river for twenty thousand years soon disappeared.

The first attempts to tame the Upper Rhine for human needs began in 1817. Until that time, the river had been left largely unaltered, allowed to meander across a wide

Salmon in the Rhine

So many salmon once lived in the Rhine that the water flashed silver from their brightly reflective scales. But salmon depend on certain natural conditions to survive, as Fred Pearce explains in the article "Greenprint for Rescuing the Rhine," in New Scientist *magazine:*

The Rhine is hostile to much wildlife, including salmon. Female salmon, returning to the river of their birth after years at sea, must bury their fertilised eggs in the gravels of shallow streams, where the water is cool, fast-flowing and rich in oxygen.... But fish swimming upstream will still find that most of their former spawning grounds have disappeared.

Once hatched, salmon fry [babies] require access to slow-flowing waters in which to grow. But these nursery habitats, too, have largely disappeared in the Rhine and its tributaries.... Alexander Raat of the Dutch Organisation for the Improvement of Inland Fisheries, says that in the upper Rhine itself "only one in every thousand former gravel beds for spawning and nurseries are left."

In Switzerland, fishermen once depended on salmon for their livelihood. A century ago an average of 150,000 of the fish were caught each year in the Netherlands and Germany. The catch had fallen to under 30,000 by 1920 and disappeared entirely after 1958. Since the mid-1980s, when experimental restocking of the Rhine began, a handful of salmon have been discovered swimming upstream. But tags revealed that most had escaped from Norwegian fish farms. Last year, 15 were found. "But none, I think, have come from the Rhine system and returned," says Raat....

[There] is a growing dispute about whether it is feasible to re-create a river fit for migrating salmon... [because] anything less than a river system fit for salmon to swim up and reproduce in will be a failure.

floodplain of forests, islands, and wetlands. But in efforts to improve the river for shipping, prevent flooding, and drain marshlands for agricultural use, engineers altered the river's course in ways that would almost instantly have serious ecological consequences.

The focus of the engineering efforts centered on the zone between Basel and Karlsruhe, where the river split into a maze of shallow, narrow, winding channels, called "meanders," that constantly formed, disappeared, and reformed along different routes. These river branches created thousands of islands while forests and meadows between the branches were often flooded, creating thriving environments for plants and animals that were unique in Europe.

This natural wonderland, however, was not conducive to humans who depended on being able to navigate the river. Even small boats were unable to easily negotiate this stretch of the Rhine where rapids, unpredictable currents, and sandbars made river travel dangerous. These moving channels were also hazardous to farms and villages during spring flood season, as Roy E. Mellor writes:

> In lower [areas], the river had built up natural embankments along its course and when the flood broke through these the consequences for man were often catastrophic. Change in the course commonly had serious consequences for settlements that could find themselves suddenly deserted by the river or else it equally suddenly appeared under their walls, while several places have experienced changes that shifted them from the right to the left bank [of the river] or visa versa.[21]

The Grand Canal of Alsace

To tame the Rhine, a German engineer, Johann Tulla, drew up a plan to force the river into one straight, single channel, a process formally known as "rectification." The building of this channel took place over the course of several decades.

By the time the river was completely rectified, more than two thousand islands, with all their distinctive wildlife, had vanished. Without its natural twists and turns, the river was sixty-two miles shorter and flowed 30 percent faster, allowing ships to move quickly through the area. Meanwhile, farmers along the newly straightened river built tall earthen dikes to permanently dry out waterlogged fields, making the land fit for cultivation. Forests of poplar, willow, and cottonwood, which depended on spring floods to survive, dried out and died within a few decades.

In the twentieth century, Tulla's rectified Rhine scheme was abandoned in favor of a new plan that featured an entirely separate canal with locks and dams. The building of this waterway, the Grand Canal d'Alsace, was undertaken by French engineers. In addition, these engineers built ten hydroelectric dams on the Rhine itself between Basel and Strasbourg, with even more plants on tributaries that flowed into the river. The waters for the canal came from the Rhine, meaning that the river carried less water between its banks. In 1950 the canal was further widened, which dropped the level of the riverbed considerably and dried out many miles of the original floodplain.

The Grand Canal d'Alsace provided many benefits. For example, the electricity generated by the dams is a very important source of nonpolluting energy and powers millions of homes, businesses, and factories throughout the region. And the canal's faster current allows barges to move quickly through the region, making the transportation of goods cheaper and easier.

The canal has created many environmental problems, however. The fast-moving water has scoured the riverbed so deeply that the river has dropped twenty-two feet below its level in 1900—the height of a two-story house. With the drop in water level, ancient underground aquifers have also dropped, drying out wells and depriving willow, oak, and elm forests of the water they need to survive. This, in turn, has affected wildlife, as Monka I. Baumgarten writes:

Many species of birds once to be seen on the Upper Rhine in large numbers, nesting, wintering or resting on their passage south, have now become rare or have disappeared altogether. The most striking example of this is the stork, the characteristic bird of Alsace, once common and much loved everywhere, which now has to be artificially re-established.[22]

A second problem caused by rectification is the increased severity of floods. In spring, floodwaters now move down the Rhine twice as fast as they did before the river was straightened. In recent decades this surge has threatened Bonn and Cologne with record floodwaters, which are 35 percent higher than they were only fifty years ago. Disastrous floods that experts predicted would occur only once in two hundred years are now expected every sixty years. Overall, the efforts to "tame" the Rhine have actually made it wilder and more unpredictable. As Martin Cohen writes in the *New Statesman & Society*:

A river highway of one main channel flowing through giant locks and hydro-plants was certainly

A cathedral in Cologne rises above meadows flooded by the nearby Rhine River.

useful for a while to the new industries of Cologne, Dusseldorf and Mannheim. But this was paid for elsewhere. The sluggish backwaters that supported wildlife and fish disappeared. The new river became a fast-flowing temperamental beast, gouging out its channels and attacking the banks.[23]

To stem this uncontrollable flow and the associated erosion, engineers continue to dump more than a half million tons of gravel into the river every year. This process is expensive, however. Moreover, the dumping of gravel further harms fish and plants in the river by smothering silt beds, sand bars, and other natural features wildlife needs to survive.

The straightening of the river had another negative effect as well. In a natural setting marshes, backwaters, reed beds, and silt banks serve to filter pollutants from water that runs into the river from farm fields and urban streets. The importance of these obliterated wetlands and marshlands is summarized by Martin Cohen:

> Wetlands reduce damage from floods, improve water quality by breaking down pollutants, refresh underground water supplies (on which forests and towns depend) and produce significant amounts of fish. . . . [Wetland functions also include] anchoring shorelines, trapping [polluting] nitrates and phosphates from fertilisers, purifying sewage, and recreational uses such as hunting and birdwatching—[this makes] them more than nature reserves, but an important part of human society.[24]

Major Water Pollution

Canals, dams, and straightened channels affect the ecology of the Rhine by altering its flow, but chemicals and other pollutants pose a serious threat to all who depend on its waters. People have been dumping human and animal waste in the Rhine since they first inhabited the river's shores. Records show that residents were complaining

A scrap heap litters a dock near the Rhine Delta in Rotterdam.

about the water quality—and smell—as long ago as the Middle Ages. In fact, the river has often been called "the largest sewer in Europe."[25] At the same time, the Rhine provides water to tens of thousands of farmers raising crops and livestock along its banks. And treated water from the river is the drinking water of more than 20 million people.

Despite this massive demand for clean water, the wide array of industries along the shores of the Rhine have been allowed to dump much of their waste into the river. Over the years, hundreds of factories have dumped nearly every chemical and pollutant known to humankind into the river, including deadly heavy metals such as cadmium, mercury, copper, lead, zinc, and chromium.

The pollution begins at the huge industrial zone in Basel, where chemical and pharmaceutical manufacturers use the river to carry away industrial waste. In Karlsruhe,

Acid Rain in the Black Forest

Water pollution is only one problem afflicting natural resources in the Rhine River valley. Acid rain caused by steel mills, chemical factories, and millions of vehicles has caused great damage to the trees in the Black Forest in southern Germany.

Acid rain is caused when fossil fuels such as coal and oil are burned, releasing sulfur dioxide and nitrogen oxide into the air. The gases combine with oxygen and water vapor and may be carried hundreds of miles from their source. The poisons fall as rain that may be nearly as acidic as vinegar. The acid rain contaminates the soil and kills plants that rely on it for nutrients.

The problems for the Black Forest began in the 1960s when the pine trees began to die. At the time, scientists were unable to explain the cause. By the 1980s the problems of acid rain were well known, but by this time over one-third of the trees in the Black Forest were damaged or dying. The beautiful green needles on the pine trees were reduced to black trunks, dead limbs, and stumps. In addition, deciduous trees such as beech and oak were also affected by acid rain, and in 1984 German researchers reported that half of the country's forests were damaged by acid rain. While steps have been taken to reverse this problem, acid rain from as far away as Russia continues to take its toll on the Black Forest.

paper factories dump bleach, chlorine, and other substances used in the making of new and recycled paper products. The chemical industry of Ludwigshafen adds its own waste while the iron, steelworks, and chemical industries of the huge Rhine-Ruhr district pile on more pollution in the form of hydrochloric acid, PCBs, and other industrial waste. These chemicals combine in ways as yet unstudied to produce a toxic stew of over two thousand known compounds. Monka I. Baumgarten details the Rhine's pollution predicament:

> Years of thoughtlessly discharging untreated domestic, industrial and shipping [waste] have done grave damage to the river's ecological equilibrium. Natural

water, and particularly running water, has a certain capacity for self-purification; but if this capacity is overtaxed by excessive pollution it "gives up" and ceases to operate. The water can then support life only to a very limited extent, or perhaps not at all. In this sense the Rhine had in many respects "given up" during the period of unrestrained industrial development after the second world war. As a result of the catastrophic reduction and poisoning of the fish stock the traditional river fisheries were destroyed. [Swimming] in the river was then prohibited on hygienic grounds.[26]

Even the relatively pristine waters of the Upper Rhine are not immune to the problems posed by water pollution. For example, local industry and agriculture together discharge sewage water equivalent to the waste of 3.2 million inhabitants into the waters of Lake Constance.

Everyone's Problem

In addition to industrial pollution and human waste, gas and oil leaking from the engines of pleasure boats, along with motor oil from land vehicles that is washed into the river continues to threaten the Rhine. Since only one gallon of gas or oil can make 1 million gallons of river water undrinkable, and cannot be easily removed from the water by conventional treatment plants, such pollution is a serious threat. Tens of thousands of leaking oil storage tanks on the riverbanks add to this threat.

Other sources of pollution are the daily activities of people who live along the Rhine. As Raymond H. Dominick III writes in *The Environmental Movement in Germany*, soap has been a major pollutant:

Oil storage tanks line a canal at Europort. Industrial pollution along the Rhine poses a serious threat to the river.

Detergent suds were the second new blight on the water. Catering to the perceived wishes of the . . . housewives, soap manufacturers had invented and marketed new detergents whose foam was almost indestructible. By 1960 newspapers featured photos of ships on Germany's canals almost buried under mounds of suds. In some places drifts of foam reached heights of more than twelve feet! . . . Aside from the obvious aesthetic problems, [the news magazine] *Der Spiegel* enumerated this daunting list of additional damage from the detergent's durable residue: interfering with commercial boat traffic, ending sport boating, endangering auto traffic on roads near waterways, fouling drinking water, crippling the performance of water purification plants, and killing the [flora and fauna] of the waterways by choking out sunlight and oxygen.[27]

While steps were taken in the 1970s to change the formula of detergents to reduce sudsing and to construct leakproof oil storage facilities, pollution has continued to pour into the Rhine. Downstream in the Netherlands, this pollution of a major source of drinking water forces most people to drink bottled water. In *The Light in Holland*, Anthony Bailey describes the situation of those who live near the end of the Rhine:

Rotterdam is [a] city washed by the river Rhine, and people who work there but live elsewhere generally bring a flask of water with them in the mornings to make their coffee or tea. Water taken from the river is kept in open basins for a month and treated with active carbon and a little chlorine [to make it drinkable], but it is never what one water expert I talked to called "top quality." In spring and summer it is much less than top. Phenols, chemicals, and sewage have left their mark. Rainier seasons help, and so does anything which reduces industrial activity on the upper Rhine and its tributaries, like the French general strike of 1968 or the collapse of Germany in 1945—two occasions when the Dutch noticed a great improvement in the quality of the water.[28]

Toxic Silt

People in the Netherlands have to deal with river pollution in another form as well. Many hazardous substances not only flow through the Rhine's waters but attach to the fine particles of silt, or sand, that are carried and deposited by the river. This toxic silt accumulates in great quantities at the Rhine Delta by the North Sea.

A variety of poisonous substances may be found in this silt, and some are the most deadly chemicals on Earth. For example, in 1995 exceedingly high levels of chemicals known as chlorinated paraffins were discovered in the Rhine Delta region. Chlorinated paraffins are used in the manufacture of paint, sealants, and adhesives, and are valued for their flame-retardant qualities in plastics production. Unfortunately, these compounds are even more toxic than dangerous poisons such as DDT, PCBs, and other by-products of the industrialized world. And chlorinated paraffins accumulate in the tissues of animals, causing cancer as well as liver and kidney damage. Known to be toxic to marine life, the chlorinated paraffins find their way into the delta silt after being discharged upstream by Hoechst, a chemical manufacturer in Germany.

The contaminated silt causes major difficulties for the Dutch, who must dredge it from their waterways to keep them open for shipping. In centuries past, this silt was spread on farm fields as fertilizer or used to fill in wetlands and lakeshores. Today, however, this silt is too polluted for such purposes and must be disposed of as toxic waste. This has forced the Dutch government to build two huge, sealed dumps along the North Sea coast where up to 55 million cubic feet of polluted silt is permanently buried. The problem does not end here, however. Space in these dumps ran out in 2002, forcing the expenditure of millions of dollars to build a new toxic dump site.

Deadly Chemical Spill

Efforts to clean up pollution in the Rhine began in the early 1970s. In 1986, however, much of the progress was undone when a massive toxic spill was released from the Sandoz Chemical plant in Basel. In the following Time *article, "A Proud River Runs Red: The Watch on the Rhine Is for Pollution," Jennifer B. Hull describes the spill:*

Last week the proud waters of Western Europe's great natural thoroughfare were contaminated, its legendary banks littered with thousands of dead fish, eels and waterfowl. The pollution was the result of a fire at Schweizerhalle, Switzerland, near Basel, in a warehouse that stored some 1,200 tons of deadly agricultural chemicals. Firemen attempting to put out the blaze accidentally washed some of the chemicals into the river, where they soon formed a 35-mile-long trail that moved downstream at 2 m.p.h.... By week's end it was clear that Western Europe was undergoing its worst ecological accident ever.

The disaster harmed thousands of Europeans. Up and down the river, villagers who depend on the Rhine for drinking water were forced to get their supplies from fire trucks. In Germany, farmers from Karlsruhe to Dusseldorf scrambled to remove livestock from grazing pastures near the river. In Strasbourg, France, sheep that drank from the Rhine died. Police in Basel and other cities banned all fishing in the river and its tributaries until further notice....

Scientists estimate that up to 30 tons of chemicals went into the Rhine, including herbicides, pesticides and fertilizers as well as some 4,000 lbs. of toxic mercury.

For the residents of Basel the accident was a nighttime terror. It was just after 3 a.m. when civil-defense sirens sounded and police cars with loudspeakers began driving down streets, warning people to keep their windows shut.... When dawn broke, the city was cloaked in a cloud of sulfurous fumes. Chemical dyes swept into the river during the fire turned the Rhine red.

Chemical Leaks

While many pollutants are intentionally dumped in the Rhine, the river has also suffered from accidental discharges that have had catastrophic consequences. The worst such disaster along the Rhine occurred in

November 1986 when a fire consumed a warehouse owned by the chemical and pharmaceutical manufacturer Sandoz AG in Basel. This storage facility was filled with chemicals, and when firefighters attempted to put out the blaze, they washed more than thirty tons of mercury and other toxins into the river. As the chemicals moved down the Rhine over the next week, more than a half million fish were killed. Meanwhile, people who lived along the river were unable to drink or even wash with the water from their home taps.

The Sandoz chemical spill reversed more than ten years of efforts to restore fish populations along the river. In the days after the accident, residents along the Rhine staged public protests against the lax safety measures employed by Sandoz. Even as these events were unfolding, it was revealed that the Swiss company Ciba-Geigy had accidentally released nine hundred pounds of highly toxic pesticides into the Rhine only hours before the Sandoz fire.

The Sandoz disaster gained worldwide attention; though smaller spills garner far less attention, the results may be nearly as tragic. In November 2001, for example, a Dutch chemical tanker caught fire and, as a result, accidentally discharged almost one hundred thousand gallons—eighteen hundred tons—of highly corrosive nitric acid in the river near the Bayer factory in the German city of Krefeld. As a cloud of orange smoke billowed from the burning ship, police warned nearby residents to keep their windows shut to keep out the toxic gases. How this chemical spill harmed the river is unknown, but nitric acid is extremely corrosive and can injure or kill organisms that come in contact with it.

The Dutch chemical tanker Stolt Rotterdam *is doused by water cannons after catching fire near Krefeld, Germany, in November 2001.*

Agricultural Problems

While industry causes problems, agriculture plays a major role in polluting the Rhine. Farmers along the Rhine annually apply tons of pesticides, herbicides, and fertilizers to their fields, and these substances wash into the river with rain and irrigation runoff. The herbicides kill microscopic plankton, the essential base of a food chain encompassing insects, fish, and birds. Meanwhile, the fertilizer causes algae to grow out of control. These huge algae "blooms" shut out light that other water plants require. At some point the algae suffer a massive die-off, and as they decay, they use up oxygen in the river that fish and plants need to survive.

Added to this toxic mix are huge quantities of animal waste that is washed into the river from hog feedlots and dairy farms. While the threat posed by agriculture is severe, few organizations address the problem. As one scientist said, "Diffuse pollution by agricultural nutrients and pesticides will remain one of the greatest threats to water quality throughout the Rhine basin. None of the Rhine basin countries has adequate government policies to deal with this problem."[29]

Another problem associated with agricultural chemicals concerns salt pollution in the form of high salinity in the water. Most of the salt dumped in the river comes from the potash mines in the Alsace region. (Potash is the name given to several compounds containing potassium, such as potassium oxide, potassium chloride, and potassium sulfates.) Potash is used mainly for the production of fertilizers, and the factories that mine and manufacture these substances dump nearly fifty thousand tons of salt into the Rhine every day—enough to fill fourteen railroad freight cars.

Water contaminated with so much salt is unusable for growing flower and vegetable crops. This is a particularly troublesome problem for farmers in the Netherlands who earn a living growing bulb flowers such as tulips, irises, daffodils, and hyacinths, which are particularly sensitive to salt. Though there have been few studies to determine the human health hazards of drinking water contaminated with high levels of salt, it is known that too much consumption of salt contributes to high blood pressure and other medical problems.

The third problem associated with agriculture concerns the use of precious river water to irrigate crops such as tomatoes and rice—water-intensive crops that would not grow in the region naturally. This practice draws so much water away from the river that experts fear that marshlands may dry out and disappear.

Flooding Fears

While water pollution is a centuries-old problem along the Rhine, a new threat—climate change—has created a new uncertainty along the river. A majority of scientists who study global warming believe that the average temperature on Earth has been gradually rising since the

A flood victim sandbags the entrance to his house in Bonn, Germany. The frequency of floods along the Rhine is increasing.

1940s, partially as a result of the burning of fossil fuels by automobiles and factories. This has influenced the environment in various ways, depending on the area. For example, large portions of southern Europe have received less rain and endured droughts in recent years. In the Rhine region, however, rainfall has increased dramatically—up to 40 percent—between the mid-1960s and the late 1990s.

European researchers believe that this increased rainfall is responsible for severe flooding along the Rhine. In December 1993 water from the Rhine poured into many towns, and thousands of people had to be evacuated to higher ground in the Cologne, Meuse, and Moselle regions.

Not only is the flooding severe, but it appears to be increasingly frequent. Before the twentieth century, such flooding was only expected every one hundred years, but a similar weather pattern caused renewed flooding along the Rhine only two years later in 1995.

Reversing the Damage

While global warming and pollution continue, millions of people who live along the Rhine are dedicated to reversing the daunting problems facing the river. And remarkable progress has been made in several areas. Some factories have reduced dumping into the river, certain regions have been reclaimed for wetlands, and thousands of farmers are reducing chemical runoff by moving to organic food production. As these steps reduce the total load of pollution flowing into the Rhine, observers hope that the river will become cleaner, not dirtier, during the coming years.

5

·········

Cleaning Up
the Rhine

The Rhine River has served the people of central Europe for millennia, providing food, natural resources, recreation, transportation, and countless other benefits. The river has also been a source of inspiration for poets, painters, composers, and everyday citizens whose lives have been immeasurably improved by simply gazing upon its peaceful flowing waters and beautiful shoreline.

For centuries, citizens along the Rhine assumed that the river was there to serve them. They considered it a dependable resource to slake their thirst, water their crops, stock their dinner tables, and carry their organic and chemical wastes to the sea. Few people questioned this assumption until the beginning of the twentieth century when the salmon began to disappear. Even then, although there were calls to clean up the river, there was little technology at the time to do so, and powerful industrial interests, economic hard times, and wars took precedence over its cleanup. As a result, the Rhine remained one of the dirtiest rivers in Europe.

Tourists enjoy the banks of the Rhine in this nineteenth-century painting. The once-revered river became one of Europe's dirtiest bodies of water.

A Growing Environmental Awareness

Until the 1950s few Europeans gave much thought to the ecology of the Rhine River. In the years immediately following World War II, a large majority of the people who lived along the river were concerned with rebuilding their nation after the devastation caused by Allied bombing. Throughout the 1950s and early sixties, however, even before the founding of the modern environmental movement, the pollution in the Rhine began to garner occasional attention in the German press, as Raymond H. Dominick III writes:

> On June 3, 1954, a banner headline in one of Germany's largest circulation general interest newspapers, the *Hamburger Abendblatt*, screamed "Water Cycle in Greatest Danger!" Testifying to the breadth of alarm, about the same time a journal catering to industrialists featured the headline "*Mangelware Wasser* (Water: A Commodity in Short Supply)." At the opposite political pole, a socialist newspaper warned its readers, "A catastrophe comes

ever closer: the collapse of our water supply." In 1960, the inflammatory *Bildzeitung* exclaimed in its typical headline two inches tall, "The Rhine Still Stinks!" adding in only slightly smaller letters, "Why is the [German congress] delaying the new Water Law?" Ten years later, the more sedate *Die Welt* headlined a report on Germany's rivers with "20 Million Drink Water from Germany's Largest Sewer," by which it meant the Rhine River.[30]

These headlines raised public awareness about the pollution of the Rhine and put politicians on notice that people expected something to be done.

The first real movement to clean up the Rhine was spearheaded by the Alliance for Protection of Germany's Waters, an organization comprising commercial and sport fishermen who saw their income and recreational opportunities diminished by pollution in the river. Noting that only three thousand salmon had been caught in the Rhine in 1956 and that those fish could not be eaten because they reeked of chemicals, the alliance brought together people from a wide spectrum of German society. Membership in the alliance grew to 1 million by the end

Oil barrels near Rotterdam. The German press first noted petroleum- and chemical-based pollution of the Rhine in the mid-1950s.

of the 1950s as scientists, politicians, industrialists, conservationists, farmers, and those in the tourism business lobbied politicians to clean up the Rhine. Throughout the 1960s the German government passed a series of laws governing the Rhine and other waterways, with notable attention given to proper disposal of used motor oil and the banning of the phospate-laden sudsy detergents that left huge piles of soapy foam in the river.

The Commission for the Protection of the Rhine

By the late 1960s environmental movements blossomed in Germany, the Netherlands, and elsewhere, and more laws were passed in those countries to protect the environment, while agencies within the national government were formed to monitor and enforce the legislation. The Dutch were particularly insistent in pushing for a cleaner environment, as Anthony Bailey writes:

> Because the Rhine is an international river, with five countries bordering it, and the Dutch at the lowest, smelliest end (and no divine power has yet shown much interest in cleaning it up), the Dutch have pushed hard for joint action. In 1950 their initiative produced the International Commission for the Protection [of the Rhine Against Pollution or ICPR], which took inventories and made reports. In 1963 the commission was given legal status and a headquarters in Coblentz, and pollution parameter limits were established. The Germans, who cause most of the pollution, have been encouraged to invest [billions of dollars] in sanitation projects. Holland has put some of its own offenders in better order... building more and better sewage-treatment plants, and forcing some factories to move if they couldn't meet stricter requirements.[31]

In addition to the Netherlands, the ICPR consisted of Germany, France, Luxembourg, and Switzerland. The first task undertaken by the ICPR was the creation of detailed analyses of the nature, extent, and sources of pollution in the Rhine. The group informed their respective governments of their findings and then proposed international treaties aimed at cleaning up the river.

Despite these efforts, the ICPR lacked political clout to pass the treaties and could not convince governments to spend the billions of dollars necessary to clean up the river. Meanwhile, water quality continued to deteriorate. By the early 1970s so much untreated sewage was flowing into the river that oxygen levels in the water declined rapidly, suffocating fish and plants. At the same time river fauna and flora were being driven toward extinction, another problem, excessive mercury and cadmium, was found in the tissues of fish that did survive. With a growing support for environmental action among the general public, the ICPR finally was able to lobby governments to spend the money needed to clean up the problem.

As a result of coordinated cleanup projects, the Rhine began a slow recovery in 1975. Industrial plants, cities, and villages built or upgraded water treatment plants to clean up their waste. By 1986 the oxygen content in the river had risen dramatically, as had the numbers of fish species.

Unfortunately, the fire and resulting chemical spill at the Sandoz plant in Switzerland resulted in extremely toxic pesticides flowing into the Rhine, reversing a decade of improvements. After hundreds of thousands of fish died from the spill, many observers once again gave up on the Rhine as a dead river. The tragedy, however, inspired the ICPR to work even harder to achieve its goals. As ICPR official Koos Wieriks stated, "the new environmental disaster helped create an atmosphere of urgency. The disaster got things moving."[32]

The Rhine Action Plan

With broad support among the general public, the commission set up a three-part, fifteen-year program called the Rhine Action Plan (RAP) in 1987. Utilizing the spill as a

Greenpeace activists, in protest of Rhine pollution, descend from a bridge above the river in Leverkusen, Germany, in 1986.

rallying point for the public, the RAP set a goal of cleaning up the Rhine to such an extent that Atlantic salmon, sea trout, shad, and sturgeon would once again be able to breed in the river by the year 2000. While such an ambitious program had earlier met resistance due to its expense, Rhineland politicians now supported it unanimously. The ICPR Salmon 2000 website states the original goal of the RAP: "The ecosystem of the Rhine must become a suitable habitat to allow the return to this great European river of the higher species which were once present here and have since disappeared (such as salmon)."[33]

To efficiently accomplish this difficult task the commission laid out specific goals to create a healthy environment for the fish, as stated on its official website:

[By 2002, the] discharge of the most important noxious substances into the Rhine is to be cut down by 50% compared with 1985.... Safety norms in industrial plants are to be tightened; a minimum surveillance of dischargers is to be installed; adequate environmental conditions must be restored for the flora and fauna typical of the Rhine, for salmon and other [migrating fish species, dams] must be equipped with fish passages and spawning grounds must be restored in the upper reaches of the tributaries.[34]

The Rhine River Project

In the early 1990s students in the Netherlands and Germany started the Rhine River Project, an environmental education venture. The aim of the project is to monitor the pollution levels along the Rhine where the schools are located and exchange the information between participating institutions. The following information about the program is taken from the Rhine River Project website:

All schools are situated along the Rhine or its side rivers.... During... geography, biology and chemistry [lessons] the students prepared a field study day. River use, geographical appearance and water quality were investigated. In this period the first contacts were also made with the students of the other participating schools....

[All] participating students went to the river to gather data about the water quality (they tested oxygen concentration, the concentration of some salts, temperature, pH and conductivity. Also a description of the weather and the location was made). The results were sent to the other participating schools through E-mail, so every school was able to use the data along the river Rhine. Pupils tried to draw conclusions about the differences in water quality along the river Rhine....

[The] participating schools agreed to the following aims:

- emphasize the role of the Rhine as an important link between countries in Europe;

- make pupils aware of the European dimension of local and national decisions on the Rhine and its environments;

- study of the influence of humans on the river-bed of the Rhine and the resulting problems on water-management;

- stressing the fact that the participants themselves have an important influence on the water quality.

To help ensure continuing cooperation from companies along the Rhine, the ICPR set up programs to test water quality while instituting pollution patrols to monitor industry along the Rhine. Many of these patrols rely on volunteers, some of whom ride their bicycles along the river looking for illegal trash dumpers and other threats to the fish. Steep fines are now in place to be levied against repeat violators.

Industry Does Its Part

Realizing that they could vastly improve their public image—and make the river cleaner—some corporations voluntarily cleaned up their waste stream. For example, German chemical producer BASF cut the pollution emanating from its huge plant in Ludwigshafen by 90 percent between 1974 and 1994. BASF and other companies also reduced dumping of major toxins such as cadmium, mercury, and other compounds by 50 to 70 percent.

Such initiatives carry a price tag. Companies investing in new production facilities now see about 40 percent of their construction costs going toward safety measures alone. Still, prevention is cheaper than cleanup. For example, Sandoz had to spend $100 million to detoxify contaminated soil to levels more than fifty feet deep after the chemical fire in 1986.

The Salmon Return

By the mid-1990s it was obvious that the ICPR's goals—once thought impossible—were being achieved. Salmon and other fish species were returning to the Rhine in greater numbers, and the programs and proposals created by the ICPR were being used as models by other nations trying to clean up their waterways. As German environmental minister Angela Merkel stated: "The rebirth of the Rhine, evidenced by the return of its salmon, has to count as one of the greatest environmental success stories of the century."[35]

The survival of the fish is aided by oxygen levels in the river water that are almost back to what is considered normal. But humans have had to help the natural process by restocking the Rhine with more than 3 million salmon. Today, naturally born salmon swim in the river next to those raised on fish farms. Spurred on by these positive

Forcing Industry to Clean Up Its Act

While politicians attempt to legislate a less polluted Rhine, the city of Rotterdam achieved its goal of a cleaner river in a short time span by hitting the polluters with lawsuits. With the threat of having to pay out millions of dollars for dumping zinc, chromium, copper, mercury, cadmium, and other toxins in the river, industries along the Rhine are cleaning up their act out of self-interest, as the following article from Chemistry and Industry *magazine points out:*

The German chemical industry is going to cut waste emissions into the Rhine river; not with the specific purpose of cleaning up the heavily polluted European artery, but rather to avoid litigation by the Dutch Port of Rotterdam. The German chemical industry association (VCI) has signed an agreement with the City of Rotterdam under which the German companies are to clean up emissions into the river, and the Port of Rotterdam is to defer possible legal action against polluters.

The trade-off is no secret. Wolfgang Munde, vice-chairman of the VCI, explained that the agreement would be beneficial to both sides. The port of Rotterdam would get a "cleaner harbour," and the German companies would be exempt from legal action.

Port of Rotterdam spokesman Rob van Dijk put it even more bluntly: "We used the threat of legal action as a means of pressuring them into the agreement". . . .

There is no altruism behind Rotterdam's harsh stand on cleaning up the Rhine. Pollution dumped into the river during its journey through the industrial heartlands of Switzerland, France, Germany and the Netherlands is causing a major headache for the port authority.

[Millions of pounds] of poisonous slurry is dredged up from the harbour annually to maintain the necessary depth. Because of the polluted state of the slurry, it has to be stored in special waste dumps. Cleaner slurry would save millions of [dollars].

developments, the ICPR has added new goals such as further reducing nitrogen, phosphorus, and mercury levels in the river by convincing agricultural and industrial polluters to produce less of these toxins.

Despite the quantifiable success, work continues on the Rhine. As biologist Gottfried Schmidt, who worked for more than twenty-five years to restore the Rhine, stated: "We haven't yet reached the point where we can sit on our hands . . . but we needn't be so very pessimistic, either. After all . . . killing a river is fast work; restoring it takes time."[36]

Riverbanks

Cleaning up the water is only one part of the ICPR program for restoration of the Rhine. In the late 1980s researchers realized that to truly restore the river they would have to do more than simply stop dumping waste into it. Healthy wetlands, meanders, and natural riverbank ecology that helped filter and clean water flowing into the river were also necessary. As Anne Schulte-Wulwer-Leidig of the secretariat of the ICPR states: "Improved water quality isn't enough. . . . We need to re-create the natural flood plains."[37]

Keeping in mind that the river is a complex ecosystem, the ICPR set up the Ecological Master Plan for the Rhine in 1991. The goal of this plan was the restoration of natural riverbank ecology that would attract birds, amphibians, beneficial insects, and fish. In some places dams and other obstacles were removed or altered to allow the fish to spawn freely on the river. The group also made proposals to prohibit building projects that would destroy any natural wetlands that remained. Martin Cohen describes the plan in detail:

> The river is being allowed to return to something approaching its natural state, with meanders, backwaters, rapids, and shallows, flooded forests and pastures and even fish ladders for the salmon [to swim past dams]. . . . More vegetation is being planted, which will help cleanse the river of its pollutants

and willow trees are being used to strengthen the banks where concrete was used. Dikes are being lowered to allow the river to overflow regularly on to new wetlands....

[In the Netherlands] engineers ... want to bulldoze the dike and allow the river the chance to return to backwaters and marshes, full of reed beds, silt banks of rushes, cress, forget-me-nots and overhanging trees. Further down the river, after centuries of pumping out lakes and building dikes to drain land for farming, the Dutch now aim to return one-sixth of the land to the floodwaters. Compromises will be made with farmers and power generators, but today the weight of the economic advantage is seen as lying with the ecologists.[38]

A boat is moored in front of a row of houses flooded by the Rhine in March, 2001.

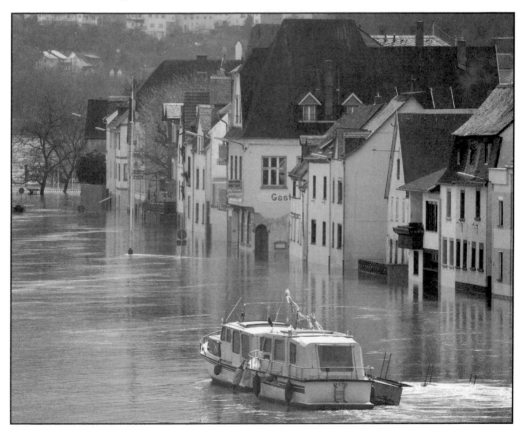

While plans reestablishing wetlands clearly benefit the river, such restoration is extremely expensive. Nevertheless, France, Germany, and the Netherlands have committed billions of dollars to the programs.

Experts point out that the restoring of the Rhine's wetlands takes not only vast amounts of money but a change in basic attitudes. As Fred Pearce explains in *New Scientist* magazine:

> For a thousand years the Dutch have reclaimed marshes, pumped dry thousands of lakes and erected dikes to keep sea and river water at bay. But now they are doing the unthinkable—bulldozing holes in their dikes and flooding fields. And they are encouraging their straightened and embanked rivers to form backwaters and penetrate the surviving marshes. The Dutch government's Master Plan for Nature was set in motion in 1990, when ecologists breached the first dike, at Duursde Waarden, a [3000-acre] nature reserve of marsh and willow forest on . . . one of three main routes that the Rhine takes to the sea. Progress so far is slow. But eventually they want to give up to 15 per cent of the Netherlands' farmland back to the flood.[39]

In 1998 Rhine restoration projects in the Netherlands were given another boost by the Fourth National Policy on Water Management meeting that called for nations to remove as many unnatural obstacles to floodwaters as possible. To further their aims, governments funded the project with about $1 billion.

German Efforts

With the Netherlands leading the way, Germany also has dedicated considerable time, money, and expertise on efforts to restore the Rhine. The Bislicher Insel Restoration Project is one of the most ambitious of these initiatives, as the land destined for reclamation was heavily used for agricultural, hunting, and recreational purposes.

The project first began purchasing land in 1982 in the Bislicher Insel area on the lower Rhine floodplain between the towns of Xantern and Wesel near the Dutch border. The group then held meetings with farmers, fishing associations, local communities, and water authorities in order to generate public support.

The group began by planting native vegetation such as black poplar, which provides quality habitat for wildlife. The plan also eliminated hunting and almost all fishing in the targeted restoration area. While this move disconcerted sports enthusiasts, the removal of two illegally located trailer parks created more controversy since it forced the removal of twenty-six hundred permanent house trailers, forcing hundreds of families to relocate. Farmers, too, were asked to make sacrifices, as cornfields were plowed

Cormorants (pictured) are among several species of birds slowly returning to the German Rhineland.

under, livestock grazing was banned from riverbanks, and a large breeding facility for thoroughbred horses was closed down and the property restored to its natural state. Meanwhile, a major highway through the area was closed, and others were reengineered for "traffic calming"—that is, obstacles such as speed bumps, stop signs, and traffic circles were added to slow cars and encourage drivers to find other routes.

The Bislicher Insel Restoration Project has proven particularly beneficial to birds that had largely abandoned the Rhine. For example, the largest cormorant colony in Germany, with more than two hundred breeding pairs counted in 1999, now exists in the area. In addition,

International Cooperation

The Rhine and the Mississippi River face similar problems. The following 1997 article by Lee Poston, "European River Managers Begin Mississippi Studies," from the Environmental News Network website, describes how European environmental engineers visited the Mississippi in 1997 to learn about American clean-up efforts:

"European river managers will study the Mississippi River basin to learn how the U.S. deals with pollution, flooding, species loss and overcrowding. In a unique exchange program, a group of European river managers...travel the Mississippi River basin from New Orleans...to Minneapolis...to learn how the United States deals with problems such as pollution, overcrowding, flooding and species loss. During the eight-day trip they will visit locks and dams, view towns and farms damaged by the 1993 floods, and tour a town buried by river sediment more than 100 years ago.

several species of birds including nightingales, mute swans, and sparrow hawks have returned to the area while bean geese and white-fronted geese have started to use the area as a winter feeding site.

Despite this success, agricultural, business, and other local interests continue to resist the project since they feel it is infringing on their rights to use the area as they had for years. Gravel and salt mining continues unabated in one area, and local governments have refused to move some dikes.

Stewards of the River

In Germany and elsewhere work to restore the river's health continues, but problems remain along the Rhine. While factories have been able to cut back on major pollutants, and cities have reduced sewage dumping, agricultural chemicals and fertilizers continue to wash into the river. As a consequence, phosphorus and nitrogen concentrations in the Rhine remain high.

These 'exchange students' are part of a World Wildlife Fund project designed to foster understanding between river managers, policy makers, flood control experts and environmentalists from both sides of the Atlantic on how best to manage two rivers—the Rhine and the Mississippi—that share similar and potentially devastating problems. Last year, a delegation from the Mississippi region visited their colleagues in the Rhine region of Germany and the Netherlands, and many of them will participate in this year's trip....

The Mississippi, one of the primary arteries of interstate and international commerce in the U.S., supports extensive breeding habitat for waterfowl and has been transformed into one of the world's primary sources of food. The environmental price tag has been high, however. Agricultural drainage, structural alterations of the river channel, and navigation and floodplain development, have led to a substantial decrease in wildlife populations, deteriorated water quality, and increased flood damages."

While accidental discharges of pollution have been reduced by the chemical industry, any mishap such as a fire, break in an oil pipeline, or tank leakage could cause great damage to the river at any time. Several tributaries that flow into the Rhine that are not targeted for restoration or protection, such as the Main, also continue to introduce pollution into the river. Despite these problems, ecologists remain hopeful for the future.

The International Commission for the Protection of the Rhine celebrated its fiftieth birthday in 2000. Since the group was founded in 1950, the Rhine has changed from "Germany's Largest Sewer" to a living river that supports salmon, pike, trout, catfish, crayfish, and even freshwater sponges. While many of these species are still struggling, there is optimism for the Rhine as the waters run cleaner with each passing year. And the ICPR now says the Rhine is one of the cleanest rivers in Europe.

The ICPR has not slowed its efforts to improve the river, however. In 2000 the commission drafted a strategy to continue restoring the Rhine through 2020. Meanwhile, a short-term program slated to end in 2005 will link flood protection with ecological restoration, including floodplain enlargement through dike removal and reconstruction of backwaters and meanders. This program is expected to cost over $5.5 billion.

With its long history of providing sustenance and wealth to those who live and work along its banks, it is fitting that, after several thousand years, people are now acting as stewards for the river. And science has proven that these efforts are not in vain. Experience has shown time and again that if treated with care, "Father Rhine" will continue to support its people for many centuries to come.

Notes

· · · · · · · ·

Chapter 1: Flowing Through Europe

1. Monk Gibbon, *The Rhine & Its Castles*. New York: W.W. Norton, 1958, p. 3.
2. Goronwy Rees, *The Rhine*. New York: G.P. Putnam's Sons, 1967, p. 50.
3. William Graves, "The Rhine: Europe's River of Legend," *National Geographic*, April, 1967, p. 474.
4. Stuart Pigott, *Touring Wine Country: The Mosel & Rheingau*. London: Reed Consumer Books, 1997, p. 9.
5. Rees, *The Rhine*, p. 107.
6. Graves, "The Rhine," p. 459.
7. Gibbon, *The Rhine & Its Castles*, pp. 3–4.

Chapter 2: History and Conflict Along the Rhine

8. Rees, *The Rhine*, p. 20.
9. Rees, *The Rhine*, p. 23.
10. Roger A. Toepfe, "Germany," www.members.aol.com/RAToepfer/webdoc7x.htm, 1998.
11. Graves, "The Rhine," p. 474.
12. Graves, "The Rhine," p. 474.
13. Paul Halsall, "Jewish History Sourcebook: The Black Death and the Jews 1348–1349 CE," July 1998. www.fordham.edu.
14. Walther Ottendorf-Simrock, *Castles on the Rhine*. Chicago: Argonaut, 1967, p. 20.
15. Quoted in Rudolph Chelminski, "The Maginot Line: Not the Blunder It's Made Out to Be," *Smithsonian*, June 1997. www.smithsonianmag.si.edu.
16. Rees, *The Rhine*, p. 29.

Chapter 3: A River of Commerce and Industry

17. Roy E. Mellor, *The Rhine: A Study in the Geography of Water Transport*. Aberdeen, Scotland: University of Aberdeen, 1983, p. 78.

18. Graves, "The Rhine," p. 461.
19. Pigott, *Touring Wine Country*, p. 12.
20. Pigott, *Touring Wine Country*, p. 9.

Chapter 4: A Struggling River

21. Mellor, *The Rhine*, p. 21.
22. Monka I. Baumgarten, *Baedeker's Rhine*. Englewood Cliffs, NJ: Prentice-Hall, 1985, p. 25.
23. Martin Cohen, "Learn Your Water Tables," *New Statesman & Society*, September 1994, p. 28.
24. Cohen, "Learn Your Water Tables," p. 28.
25. Quoted in Baumgarten, *Baedeker's Rhine*, p. 22.
26. Quoted in Baumgarten, *Baedeker's Rhine*, p. 24.
27. Raymond H. Dominick III, *The Environmental Movement in Germany*. Bloomington: Indiana University Press, 1992, p. 141.
28. Anthony Bailey, *The Light in Holland*. New York: Alfred A. Knopf, 1970, p. 91.
29. Water Treatment of the Netherlands, Department of Public Works and Water Management, Institute for Inland Water Management and Waste, "Visions for the Rhine," 2000. www.worldwatercouncil.org.

Chapter 5: Cleaning Up the Rhine

30. Dominick, *The Environmental Movement in Germany*, pp. 139–40.
31. Bailey, *The Light in Holland*, pp. 91–92.
32. Quoted in Page Chichester, "Resurrection on the Rhine," *International Wildlife*, September/October 1997, p. 2.
33. International Commission for the Protection of the Rhine, "Towards the Goal: Salmon 2000," *ICPR—Salmon 2000*. www.iksr.org.
34. International Commission for the Protection of the Rhine, "Towards the Goal: Salmon 2000."
35. Quoted in Chichester, "Resurrection on the Rhine," p. 28.
36. Quoted in Chichester, "Resurrection on the Rhine," p. 28.
37. Quoted in Fred Pearce, "Greenprint for Rescuing the Rhine," *New Scientist*, June 26, 1993.
38. Cohen, "Learn Your Water Tables," p. 28.
39. Fred Pearce, "Greenprint for Rescuing the Rhine."

For Further Reading

Christopher J. Anderson and John P. Langellier, *The Fall of Fortress Europe: From the Battle of the Bulge to the Crossing of the Rhine*. New York: Chelsea House, 2001. The story of the bitter World War II battles along the Rhine as the Allies attempted to cross the river in the face of vigorous German defenses.

C.A.R. Hills, *The Rhine*. Morristown, NJ: Silver Burdett, 1979. Life and history along the Rhine illustrated with dozens of photographs.

Michael Pollard, *The Rhine*. New York: Benchmark Books, 1998. The story of the Rhine from its ancient birth to its modern life as an industrial, agricultural, and scenic waterway.

Works Consulted

Books

Anthony Bailey, *The Light in Holland*. New York: Alfred A. Knopf, 1970. An interesting read on the people, history, and culture of the Netherlands.

Monka I. Baumgarten, *Baedeker's Rhine*. Englewood Cliffs, NJ: Prentice-Hall, 1985. An informative travel guide with facts, figures, and information about history, nature, the wine regions, and castles along the Rhine.

Raymond H. Dominick III, *The Environmental Movement in Germany*. Bloomington: Indiana University Press, 1992. A scholarly history of pollution in Germany and the powerful environmental movement that flourished in that country between 1871 and 1971.

Monk Gibbon, *The Rhine & Its Castles*. New York: W.W. Norton, 1958. A travelogue of the Middle Rhine region famous for its white wine, artistic culture, and castles.

Mark T. Hooker, *The History of Holland*. Westport, CT: Greenwood Press, 1999. The geography, economy, history, and culture of the Netherlands.

Walter Marsden, *The Rhineland*. New York: Hastings House, 1973. A travelogue and historical exploration of the Rhineland from the Cologne region to the Alps.

Roy E. Mellor, *The Rhine: A Study in the Geography of Water Transport*. Aberdeen, Scotland: University of Aberdeen, 1983. A scholarly study of the Rhine as it was used for shipping products and people throughout history.

Walther Ottendorf-Simrock, *Castles on the Rhine*. Chicago: Argonaut, 1967. A small book with black-and-white photos and detailed histories of dozens of castles along the Rhine, many of them built in the thirteenth and fourteenth centuries.

Stuart Pigott, *Touring Wine Country: The Mosel & Rheingau*. London: Reed Consumer Books, 1997. A travel guide to the wine country along the Rhine near the confluence of the Moselle River.

Roland Recht, *The Rhine: Culture and Landscape at the Heart of Europe*. London: Thames & Hudson, 2001. The history of the Rhine as told by authors, painters, and composers with dozens of pictures and photos of the most scenic areas along the river's course.

Goronwy Rees, *The Rhine*. New York: G.P. Putnam's Sons, 1967. The Rhine River from its headwaters in the Swiss Alps to its delta at the North Sea.

Felizia Seyd, *The Rhine*. Garden City, NY: Country Life, 1955. A tribute to the beauty and power of the Rhine with information about the major towns along its banks.

Periodicals

Chemistry and Industry, "Germans Sign Clean-Up Pact," September 2, 1991.

Page Chichester, "Resurrection on the Rhine," *International Wildlife*, September/October 1997.

Martin Cohen, "Learn Your Water Tables," *New Statesman & Society*, September 1994.

William Graves, "The Rhine: Europe's River of Legend," *National Geographic*, April 1967.

Jennifer B. Hull, "A Proud River Runs Red: The Watch on the Rhine Is for Pollution," *Time*, November 24, 1986.

Fred Pearce, "Greenprint for Rescuing the Rhine," *New Scientist*, June 26, 1993.

Internet Sources

Rudolph Chelminski, "The Maginot Line: Not the Blunder It's Made Out to Be," *Smithsonian*, June 1997. www.smithsonianmag.si.edu.

Diether Etzel, "The Barbarians," The Barbarians website, www.art1.condor.com.

Paul Halsall, "Jewish History Sourcebook: The Black Death and the Jews 1348–1349 CE," July 1998. www.fordham.edu.

Helmut Hass, "Rhine River Project Basic Information,"
    Information Rhine River Project. http://www.fh-koblenz.de.

International Commission for the Protection of the Rhine,
    "Towards the Goal: Salmon 2000," *ICPR—Salmon 2000.*
    www.iksr.org.

PortofRotterdam.com, "Port of Rotterdam—About the Port,"
    2000–01. www.portmanagement.com.

Lee Poston, "European River Managers Begin Mississippi
    Studies," *Environmental News Network,* September 19, 1997.
    www.enn.com.

Wilhelm Ruland, "Wilhelm Ruland. Legends of the Rhine. Lorelei."
    www.kellscraft.com/LegendsRhine/legendsrhine068.html,
    1999–2002. A poetic description of the Lorelei taken from the
    1906 book that was a best-seller in Germany.

Roger A. Toepfe, "Germany," www.members.aol.com/RAToepfer/
    webdoc7x.htm, 1998.

Water Treatment of the Netherlands, Department of Public Works
    and Water Management, Institute for Inland Water
    Management and Waste, "Visions for the Rhine."
    www.worldwatercouncil.org.

Index

Picture Credits

About the Author

- -

Stuart A. Kallen is the author of more than 150 nonfiction books for children and young adults. He has written on topics ranging from the theory of relativity to rock and roll history. In addition, Kallen has written award-winning children's videos and television scripts. In his spare time, the author is a singer/songwriter/guitarist in San Diego, California.